Layers of Learning
Year One • Unit One

Mesopotamia

Maps & Globes

Planets

Cave Art

Published by HooDoo Publishing
United States of America
First edition © 2014 Layers of Learning
Second edition © 2017 Layers of Learning
Copies of maps or activities may be made for a particular family or classroom. All other rights reserved. Printed in the United States of America.
(Grilled Cheese BTN Font) © Fontdiner - www.fontdiner.com
ISBN # 978-1542974042

If you wish to reproduce or print excerpts of this publication, please contact us at contact@layers-of-learning.com for permission. Thank you for respecting copyright laws.

Units at a Glance: Topics For All Four Years of the Layers of Learning Program

1	History	Geography	Science	The Arts
1	Mesopotamia	Maps & Globes	Planets	Cave Paintings
2	Egypt	Map Keys	Stars	Egyptian Art
3	Europe	Global Grids	Earth & Moon	Crafts
4	Ancient Greece	Wonders	Satellites	Greek Art
5	Babylon	Mapping People	Humans in Space	Poetry
6	The Levant	Physical Earth	Laws of Motion	List Poems
7	Phoenicians	Oceans	Motion	Moral Stories
8	Assyrians	Deserts	Fluids	Rhythm
9	Persians	Arctic	Waves	Melody
10	Ancient China	Forests	Machines	Chinese Art
11	Early Japan	Mountains	States of Matter	Line & Shape
12	Arabia	Rivers & Lakes	Atoms	Color & Value
13	Ancient India	Grasslands	Elements	Texture & Form
14	Ancient Africa	Africa	Bonding	African Tales
15	First North Americans	North America	Salts	Creative Kids
16	Ancient South America	South America	Plants	South American Art
17	Celts	Europe	Flowering Plants	Jewelry
18	Roman Republic	Asia	Trees	Roman Art
19	Christianity	Australia & Oceania	Simple Plants	Instruments
20	Roman Empire	You Explore	Fungi	Composing Music

2	History	Geography	Science	The Arts
1	Byzantines	Turkey	Climate & Seasons	Byzantine Art
2	Barbarians	Ireland	Forecasting	Illumination
3	Islam	Arabian Peninsula	Clouds & Precipitation	Creative Kids
4	Vikings	Norway	Special Effects	Viking Art
5	Anglo Saxons	Britain	Wild Weather	King Arthur Tales
6	Charlemagne	France	Cells & DNA	Carolingian Art
7	Normans	Nigeria	Skeletons	Canterbury Tales
8	Feudal System	Germany	Muscles, Skin, Cardio	Gothic Art
9	Crusades	Balkans	Digestive & Senses	Religious Art
10	Burgundy, Venice, Spain	Switzerland	Nerves	Oil Paints
11	Wars of the Roses	Russia	Health	Minstrels & Plays
12	Eastern Europe	Hungary	Metals	Printmaking
13	African Kingdoms	Mali	Carbon Chemistry	Textiles
14	Asian Kingdoms	Southeast Asia	Non-metals	Vivid Language
15	Mongols	Caucasus	Gases	Fun With Poetry
16	Medieval China & Japan	China	Electricity	Asian Arts
17	Pacific Peoples	Micronesia	Circuits	Arts of the Islands
18	American Peoples	Canada	Technology	Indian Legends
19	The Renaissance	Italy	Magnetism	Renaissance Art I
20	Explorers	Caribbean Sea	Motors	Renaissance Art II

www.Layers-of-Learning.com

3	History	Geography	Science	The Arts
1	Age of Exploration	Argentina & Chile	Classification & Insects	Fairy Tales
2	The Ottoman Empire	Egypt & Libya	Reptiles & Amphibians	Poetry
3	Mogul Empire	Pakistan & Afghanistan	Fish	Mogul Arts
4	Reformation	Angola & Zambia	Birds	Reformation Art
5	Renaissance England	Tanzania & Kenya	Mammals & Primates	Shakespeare
6	Thirty Years' War	Spain	Sound	Baroque Music
7	The Dutch	Netherlands	Light & Optics	Baroque Art I
8	France	Indonesia	Bending Light	Baroque Art II
9	The Enlightenment	Korean Peninsula	Color	Art Journaling
10	Russia & Prussia	Central Asia	History of Science	Watercolors
11	Conquistadors	Baltic States	Igneous Rocks	Creative Kids
12	Settlers	Peru & Bolivia	Sedimentary Rocks	Native American Art
13	13 Colonies	Central America	Metamorphic Rocks	Settler Sayings
14	Slave Trade	Brazil	Gems & Minerals	Colonial Art
15	The South Pacific	Australasia	Fossils	Principles of Art
16	The British in India	India	Chemical Reactions	Classical Music
17	The Boston Tea Party	Japan	Reversible Reactions	Folk Music
18	Founding Fathers	Iran	Compounds & Solutions	Rococo
19	Declaring Independence	Samoa & Tonga	Oxidation & Reduction	Creative Crafts I
20	The American Revolution	South Africa	Acids & Bases	Creative Crafts II

4	History	Geography	Science	The Arts
1	American Government	USA	Heat & Temperature	Patriotic Music
2	Expanding Nation	Pacific States	Motors & Engines	Tall Tales
3	Industrial Revolution	U.S. Landscapes	Energy	Romantic Art I
4	Revolutions	Mountain West States	Energy Sources	Romantic Art II
5	Africa	U.S. Political Maps	Energy Conversion	Impressionism I
6	The West	Southwest States	Earth Structure	Impressionism II
7	Civil War	National Parks	Plate Tectonics	Post Impressionism
8	World War I	Plains States	Earthquakes	Expressionism
9	Totalitarianism	U.S. Economics	Volcanoes	Abstract Art
10	Great Depression	Heartland States	Mountain Building	Kinds of Art
11	World War II	Symbols & Landmarks	Chemistry of Air & Water	War Art
12	Modern East Asia	The South	Food Chemistry	Modern Art
13	India's Independence	People of America	Industry	Pop Art
14	Israel	Appalachian States	Chemistry of Farming	Modern Music
15	Cold War	U.S. Territories	Chemistry of Medicine	Free Verse
16	Vietnam War	Atlantic States	Food Chains	Photography
17	Latin America	New England States	Animal Groups	Latin American Art
18	Civil Rights	Home State Study I	Instincts	Theater & Film
19	Technology	Home State Study II	Habitats	Architecture
20	Terrorism	America in Review	Conservation	Creative Kids

Unit 1-1 Printable Pack

This unit includes printables at the end. To make life easier for you we also created digital printable packs for each unit. To retrieve your printable pack for Unit 1-1, please visit

www.layers-of-learning.com/digital-printable-packs/

Put the printable pack in your shopping cart and use this coupon code:

1119UNIT1-1

Your printable pack will be free.

Layers of Learning Introduction

This is part of a series of units in the Layers of Learning homeschool curriculum, including the subjects of history, geography, science, and the arts. Children from 1st through 12th can participate in the same curriculum at the same time - family school style.

The units are intended to be used in order as the basis of a complete curriculum (once you add in a systematic math, reading, and writing program). You begin with Year 1 Unit 1 no matter what ages your children are. Spend about 2 weeks on each unit. You pick and choose the activities within the unit that appeal to you and read the books from the book list that are available to you or find others on the same topic from your library. We highly recommend that you use the timeline in every history section as the backbone. Then flesh out your learning with reading and activities that highlight the topics you think are the most important.

Alternatively, you can use the units as activity ideas to supplement another curriculum in any order you wish. You can still use them with all ages of children at the same time.

When you've finished with Year One, move on to Year Two, Year Three, and Year Four. Then begin again with Year One and work your way through the years again. Now your children will be older, reading more involved books, and writing more in depth. When you have completed the sequence for the second time, you start again on it for the third and final time. If your student began with Layers of Learning in 1st grade and stayed with it all the way through she would go through the four year rotation three times, firmly cementing the information in her mind in ever increasing depth. At each level you should expect increasing amounts of outside reading and writing. High schoolers in particular should be reading extensively, and if possible, participating in discussion groups.

These icons will guide you in spotting activities and books that are appropriate for the age of child you are working with. But if you think an activity is too juvenile or too difficult for your kids, adjust accordingly. The icons are not there as rules, just guides.

- ☺ 1st-4th
- ☺ 5th-8th
- ☺ 9th-12th

Within each unit we share:

EXPLORATIONS, activities relating to the topic;
EXPERIMENTS, usually associated with science topics;
EXPEDITIONS, field trips;
EXPLANATIONS, teacher helps or educational philosophies.

In the sidebars we also include Additional Layers, Famous Folks, Fabulous Facts, On the Web, and other extra related topics that can take you off on tangents, exploring the world and your interests with a bit more freedom. The curriculum will always be there to pull you back on track when you're ready.

www.layers-of-learning.com

MESOPOTAMIA - MAPS & GLOBES - PLANETS - CAVE PAINTINGS

UNIT ONE

MESOPOTAMIA - MAPS & GLOBES - PLANETS - CAVE PAINTINGS

*The world is so full of a number of things
I'm sure we should all be as happy as kings.*
-Robert Louis Stevenson

LIBRARY LIST

HISTORY	Search for: Mesopotamia, Sumer, Fertile Crescent, Gilgamesh, Ur, Ziggurats, and Hammurabi. ☺ ☺ ☺ Mesopotamia by Philip Steele. From DK publishers, packed full of pictures, illustrations and information for middle grades and up, or skim through with a younger child. ☺ Mesopotamia by Jane Shuter. Excavating the Past series. ☺ ☺ The Golden Sandal by Rebecca Hickox. A Cinderella story from the Middle East. ☺ ☺ The City of Rainbows by Karen Foster. Re-telling of an ancient tale from Sumer. The second half of the book containing the explanations of the tale is every bit as valuable and worthwhile as the tale itself. Fascinating. ☺ ☺ ☺ Gilgamesh the King by Ludmila Zeman: a retelling of an ancient tale from Sumer, the oldest known writings in the world. Read aloud. See the next two volumes in this trilogy as well. ☺ ☺ Gilgamesh the Hero by Geraldine McCaughrean. A retelling of the ancient tale. For middle grades and up. ☺ ☺ Hammurabi: Babylonian Ruler by Christine Mayfield and Kristine M. Quinn. Biography of an ancient Sumerian King ☺ Gilgamesh: A New English Version by Stephen Mitchell, translator. This is by far the easiest to understand version, though it does depart from strict scholarship.
GEOGRAPHY	Search for: Globes, maps, map projections, hemispheres ☺ ☺ Maps and Globes by Jack Knowlton, our favorite geography writer for kids. We love the illustrations by Harriet Bartman! ☺ ☺ My World and Globe by Ira Wolfman. Includes an inflatable globe with only the bare bones plus dozens of stickers and a magic marker to customize and personalize. ☺ ☺ Humpty Dumpty Sat on the Globe by Fereydoun Kian. Stories that help kids learn the shapes of countries and continents with easy and fun memory devices. A wonderful introduction to give kids a familiarity with our world. Great for young kids (and their parents). ☺ ☺ ☺ Geography Songs by Larry and Kathy Troxel. Use for all four years as we explore continents and countries around the globe. Big aid in memorizing. ☺ ☺ The Tarquin Globe by Gerald Jenkins and Magdalen Bear. A paper model of a globe you can buy and put together. Perfect for older kids who enjoy doing projects with their hands.

Mesopotamia - Maps & Globes - Planets - Cave Paintings

Science

Search for: Planets, space, solar system

☺ <u>Solar System</u> from Golden Books. A simple first look at the Solar System for young kids.

☺ <u>My Place in Space</u> by Robin and Sally Hirst. A witty look at where we live in the universal scheme of things.

☺ ☺ <u>Bill Nye the Science Guy: Planets</u> movie. Entertaining and fun for kids from pre-school through middle school.

☺ ☺ <u>Eyewitness: Planets</u> movie. Amazing camera work and great information from this series of movies.

☺ ☺ <u>The Magic School Bus: Lost in the Solar System</u> by Joanna Cole. If you buy one book on the solar system, this one should be it. Entertaining, great illustrations, and awesome information for young kids.

☺ ☺ <u>Our Solar System</u> by Seymour Simon. A thorough, but kid-friendly look at the solar system. Simon also has individual books about each one of the planets that are excellent.

☺ ☺ <u>How the Universe Works</u> by Heather Couper and Nigel Henbest: from Reader's Digest. Contains tons of information and amazing advanced projects to be used throughout the astronomy section

☺ <u>A Brief History of Time</u> by Stephen Hawking. A popular level book on astronomy by one of the premier astronomer/physicists in the world. Get the illustrated version if you can.

☺ <u>On the Revolutions of the Heavenly Spheres</u> by Nicholas Copernicus. This is the book that caused such an outcry from the church during the Renaissance.

The Arts

Search for: cave paintings, Lascaux

☺ <u>The Secret Cave</u> by Emily Arnold McCully. Another story of how Lascaux cave was found. The illustrations in this book are works of art in themselves.

☺ <u>The Cave Painter of Lascaux</u> by Roberta Angeletti. A school girl gets lost on a guided tour of the caves and gets a personal tour from an actual cave man. Picture book.

☺ ☺ <u>Discovery in the Cave</u> by Mark Dubowski. A level 4 easy reader, describing the discovery of the Lascaux cave.

☺ ☺ <u>Art Explained</u> from DK. Covers the whole scope of the human art endeavor from ancient times through modern art. Use this book through all four years.

☺ ☺ <u>Painters of the Caves</u> by Patricia Lauber. From National Geographic, the best part of this book is the full color pictures on every page.

☺ <u>The Cave Painters</u> by Gregory Curtis. For high school and adults, discusses the various theories about the whys and wherefores of ancient European cave art.

MESOPOTAMIA - MAPS & GLOBES - PLANETS - CAVE PAINTINGS

HISTORY: MESOPOTAMIA

Teaching Tip
Start a notebook to keep your projects in. Include tabs labeled "History," "Geography," "Science," "Writing," and "The Arts."

Fabulous Fact
The Fertile Crescent is a region in western Asia. It is situated between the mountains of Arabia to the north and the Arabian Desert to the south.

Mesopotamia is only the area around the Tigris and Euphrates Rivers.

Fabulous Fact
Mesopotamians invented a number system based on the number 60. We divide our hours into 60 minutes and our minutes into 60 seconds because of the Mesopotamians.

The farms of Mesopotamia and the Fertile Crescent may or may not have been the first on earth, but they are one of the earliest places where we know for sure that civilization flourished.

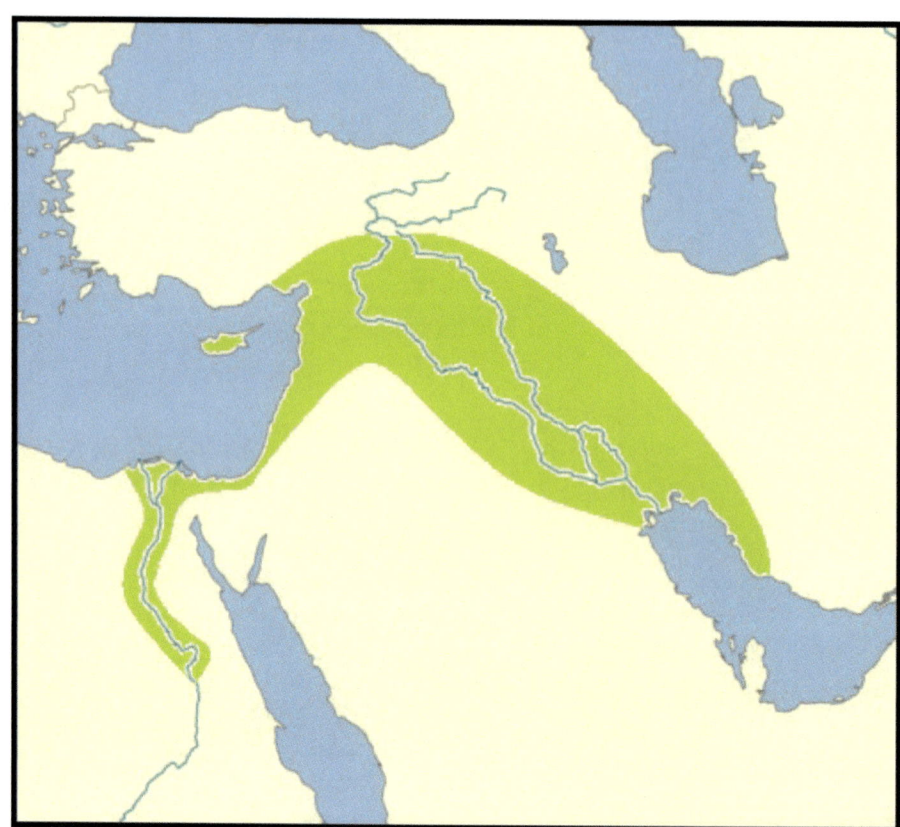

The Fertile Crescent is the area between the Tigris and Euphrates Rivers extending up north and then curving back south along the Mediterranean in what is now Israel. Archaeologists think this may be a place of very early civilization, which means a place where people first settled down and built homes. Situated between the Tigris and the Euphrates Rivers where there was plenty of fresh water, it was an ideal place for farming and starting a budding society of people.

At first, as cities began to grow they were independent city states. Each city, together with the surrounding countryside, was its own country. The two earliest loosely united countries that we know of in the Mesopotamian area were Sumer in the south and Akkad in the north. They fought back and forth between each other for centuries until finally Sumer overcame Akkad. Sumer, in turn, was overrun by the Ammorites who were overrun by the Babylonians and so on through history.

How do a bunch of independent family or tribal groups be-

Mesopotamia - Maps & Globes - Planets - Cave Paintings

come a city and then a nation? First, you have to find a good place where you can stay and farm food year after year. That means you need water. The earliest civilizations were found near fresh water. The first farms were made possible because of these water sources and the first farmers realizing how to collect seeds, plant and care for them, and produce a consistent harvest. They also built a system of canals to carry the water to the fields.

Next, you need technology advanced enough to allow you to produce more food than your family can use alone. You need irrigation, plows, scythes, wheels, and so on. If there is extra food, then not everybody has to be a farmer anymore. Some people can be weavers while others can be scribes. Some people can make jewelry or weapons or tools, and others can trade with neighboring cities.

All those people living so close together can cause problems though. Pretty soon you have thieves or dishonest businessmen, and so you need a government to make rules and punish wrongdoers. Before you know it you have a city state.

This is a mosaic from Ur showing scenes of everyday life.

Sumerians were probably very much like modern people are today, but with different stuff. They worked and played, had families, and knew both grief and joy. They lived in either reed huts or in mud brick homes. They learned to write and record their thoughts for others to read. They wrote records of how many animals were sold, how much they paid in taxes, or how big their crop was. They also wrote down poems and stories and new information about all kinds of topics. Under the sand in the modern country of Iraq archaeologists have found many of their clay tablets preserved through the millenia for us to read now.

☺ ☺ ☺ **EXPLORATION: Fertile Crescent Map**
Make copies of the Fertile Crescent map found at the end of this unit. Color the area right around the rivers green and the outly-

Additional Layer

Learn more about archeology and how we know so much about the distant past. A great book for adults or high schoolers is *Gods, Graves and Scholars: The Story of Archeology* by C.W. Ceram.

Also check out *Bill Nye the Science Guy: Archeology*, a movie for young kids.

Fabulous Fact

This is an ancient Sumerian clay tablet from about 2500 B.C.

It is an accounting to the governor about the silver in the treasury.

Teaching Tip

Have students use colored pencils and black ink pens to do map work. This will help their maps be tidy and legible so you can keep them and refer back to them throughout the unit as you're discussing.

Mesopotamia - Maps & Globes - Planets - Cave Paintings

Writer's Workshop

The *Tale of Gilgamesh* was the first recorded superhero story. It is an epic poem about a mythological hero-king named Gilgamesh. It was written on 12 tablets. Make up your own superhero. What is your superhero's name? What powers does she have? Does he have any weaknesses? Where does she live? What does he like to eat? What does she wear?

Do a character sketch in your writer's notebook about your superhero. Start by drawing a picture of your hero, then surround the picture with lots of descriptions about what the hero is like and what he can do. You may want to continue on and write a story about your superhero when you're finished with your character sketch.

Fabulous Fact

Cuneiform is wedge shaped because the stylus used to create it left that shape of impression in the clay.

"Cuneiform" comes from the Latin *cuneus*, which means "wedge."

ing areas brown. The green represents land irrigated by the river and the brown is arid land. Note that some of the areas you'll color brown are actually irrigated and used for farm land, but that you are highlighting the fertile crescent in particular.

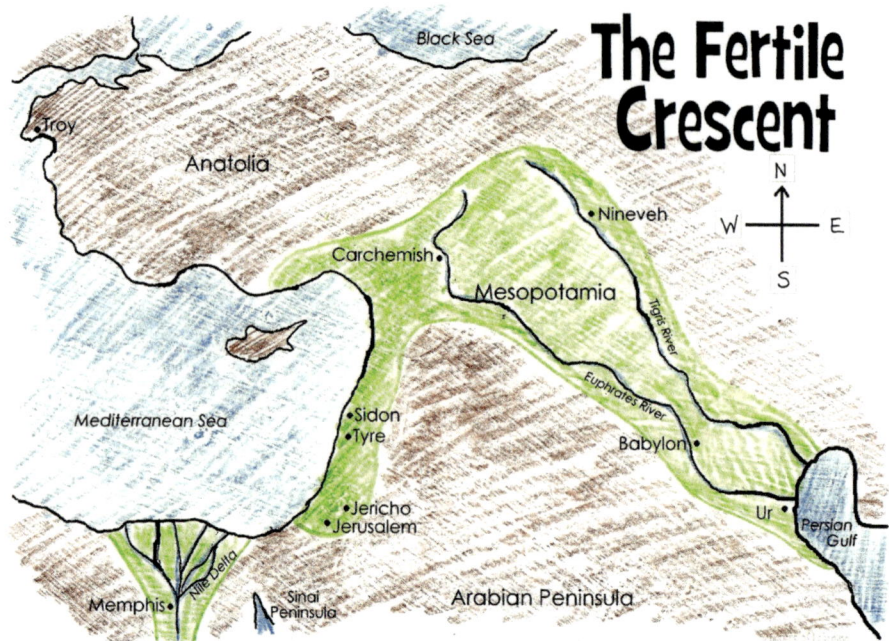

EXPLANATION: Mapping To Learn

Maps are useful learning tools because they give a relational understanding of the situation. You can see which countries were neighboring, and where the river was, and why there were no cities in the desert. Nearly all of the history units will have historical map work. Discussing the map is key to understanding it, so point things out, ask questions, and identify important areas on every map you complete.

Encourage your students to be neat and make their work readable. Younger students can do less independent labeling than older students. You may want to write or type the labels on bits of paper and let younger kids glue them on so they can join in too. You can also write them in yellow pen and let little ones trace over the words.

☺ ☺ EXPLORATION: Cuneiform Writing

Read the tale of Gilgamesh out loud and ask your student to repeat it back word for word. How important is writing? It would be hard just to remember your grocery list. What else do we use writing for all the time? Writing in Mesopotamia was done on clay tablets with a reed. Archaeologists have found many of these clay tablets and deciphered what they wrote in cuneiform.

Mesopotamia - Maps & Globes - Planets - Cave Paintings

Tale of Gilgamesh

The great hero Gilgamesh, king of Erech, was handsome and strong, but he was also cruel and tyrannical over the people of his city. The people of the city begged the gods for help, and they sent Enkidu, a man of enormous strength, to contend with Gilgamesh. Enkidu met Gilgamesh and they fought a mighty battle which Gilgamesh won. But instead of becoming enemies the two became friends. They traveled over the world together searching for adventure. They killed Humumba, the fire-breathing guardian of the cedar forest. They killed the Bull of Heaven. But the gods were angry with them for this and they decided that Enkidu must die to pay for his sin. Gilgamesh sorrowed for his friend and feared death himself. He went on a quest to discover the secret to immortality. After many adventures he finally found the secret in a thorny fragrant plant of youth that could be found only on the bottom of the sea. Gilgamesh retrieved the plant, but on his way home a snake swallowed the plant and so Gilgamesh's quest had been in vain.

Try it yourself. Get a piece of clay or play dough and flatten it into a sheet. Use a thin stick, like a skewer, a toothpick, or a craft stick to write with on the clay. Sumerians made marks by pressing the edge of the reed into the clay instead of trying to drag the reed across the clay. Can you tell why they used this method? After the scribe was done writing they fired (or dried) the clay, making

3 Essentials of A Unit:

The lesson – This is when we do our maps, timelines, reading, and discussions.

The hands-on – Do something to cement the knowledge.

The narration – No matter their age, kids should write about what they learned.

Additional Layer

Scholars have been able to translate the clay tablets, but that doesn't mean they understand everything they translate. For example, we can see that samidu is an ingredient in many recipes, but no one knows what it is. We speculate that it's a spice.

Just for fun, try several Middle Eastern spices like allspice or turmeric. One of them may just be samidu!

Additional Layer

We don't typically use seals like the Mesopotamians, but we use signatures. Practice your signature. Everyone has a unique way of signing their name, it is something that is just yours. Practice until you get it just the way you like it.

9

MESOPOTAMIA - MAPS & GLOBES - PLANETS - CAVE PAINTINGS

Writer's Workshop
Create your own cookbook with recipes that are your favorites. Along with the recipe you might even include some stories about special traditions or memories you have about food in your family.

On The Web
Here's a Mesopotamian choose-your-own-adventure tale, A Tale of Three Merchants: http://www.mesopotamia.co.uk/trade/story/sto_set.html

Fabulous Fact
Mesos means "in between" or "middle."

Potomos means "river."

Can you think of another word, besides Mesopotamia, that comes from the Greek word potomos?

Here's a hint:

On the Web
Visit the British Museum's Mesopotamia site. http://www.mesopotamia.co.uk/

it permanent. Thousands of these clay tablets have been discovered in what is now Iraq. Most of the writing consists of lists and accounts, but there have also been recipes and stories found. The most famous story is the *Tale of Gilgamesh* from Sumer.

EXPLANATION: Writer's Notebook
Give each student a writer's notebook. This is notebook they can use to jot down thoughts, write ideas, make character sketches, create stories, and just start writing! The spelling and grammar don't need to be perfect in this notebook. It is about ideas, not polished work. Writers may want to decorate the covers of their notebook to reflect themselves. Everyone should have one and use it nearly everyday. Don't be afraid to write in all different ways-- write current events, jot down a recipe, write the lyrics to a song. Look back through it often to get ideas for other writing you want to do. Tape photos or draw pictures in it. Doodle, cross out, make lists, scribble. Make it yours.

☺ ☺ **EXPLORATION: Flat Bread Feast**
We've found many clay tablets with recipes on them from Mesopotamia. They didn't have grocery stores or a lot of the ingredients we have, so all the food they made was really basic. One of their meals would have been goat stew and flat bread. You probably won't want to try the goat stew, but here's the recipe just in case:

Stew of a Kid (Baby Goat)
Head, legs, and tail should be singed before putting them in the pot to boil. Bring water to a boil. Add fat, onions, samidu, leeks, garlic, some goat's blood, and some fresh cheese. Beat them all together.

One of the earliest things people grew was wheat. Most people still eat more wheat than almost anything else. Have you ever seen a wheat seed before it is made into flour? Get wheat kernels, grind them in your blender and make flat bread (bread without yeast) out of them. You can buy wheat berries online if you can't find them locally.

Ancient Flat Bread
14 oz. flour (or ground up wheat)
1 cup water
½ teaspoon salt

Mix the water, flour, and salt together. Then knead the dough and form it into flat, round, patties. Cover it with a cloth and let it sit overnight. Bake it in an oven at 350 degrees F for 30 minutes.

Mesopotamia - Maps & Globes - Planets - Cave Paintings

You can try some honey on your bread too. Or you can put raw onions on it like the Mesopotamians did.

Modern women in Tamuz, Iraq making flat bread like their ancestors have for thousands of years. Photo by James Gordon, CC license, Wikimedia.

☺ ☺ EXPEDITION: Down on the Farm
Visit a farm to see where your food comes from. Today so much food is produced on each farm that very few people have to produce food, while the rest of us can specialize in other areas. This is how cities grow today and it's how the cities of ancient Mesopotamia grew as well.

☺ EXPLORATION: Ziggurat Builders
Ziggurats are pyramids with stepped sides, the remains of which have been found in Mesopotamia. They were not tombs like Egyptian pyramids, but were temples, which they considered to

---

Additional Layer

The type of homes we build depends on the climate we live in, as well as the natural building materials that are available.

How would it be to live in Arizona in an igloo? How about a dugout in Florida? Would a mud brick home work everywhere in the world?

On the Web

Watch this short video introduction for younger kids: "Mesopotamia: From Nomads to Farmers": https://www.youtube.com/watch?v=Ki8S5I83Ccc

Additional Layer

Mesopotamia is known as a "cradle of civilization". It is a place where cities first appeared and kings first ruled. Writing and the domestication of animals are seen as signs of civilization.

The Indus river valley in India, the Nile river, and the Yellow river valley in China are other places considered cradles of civilization. Norte Chico in South America and the Yucatan Peninsula of Central America have more recently been identified as cradles of civilization.

Mesopotamia - Maps & Globes - Planets - Cave Paintings

Deep Thoughts

Ziggurats were the highest buildings in Mesopotamian society. What are our tallest buildings? Do they reflect our values?

Additional Layer

Learn how pyramid structures have been used all over the world in different cultures for different things.

You might check out Egyptian Pyramids, Mayan Pyramids, modern pyramids and more.

Photo by Carlos Delgado; CC-BY-SA

literally be the homes of their gods. They were usually built on a hill or in a conspicuous place within the city so everyone could see and admire the ziggurat, their most important building. The temple was the smallest building at the top of the ziggurat. Make a model ziggurat from clay. Alternately, you could use sugar cubes, milk cartons, or styrofoam to build with.

☺ ☻ EXPLORATION: Cylinder Seals

To make a document official, instead of signing their name, the ancient people of Mesopotamia sealed the document or letter with a seal which they would press into the still wet clay. At first they used small square or oblong seals. Later they began to use cylinder seals that could be rolled onto the wet clay instead of pressed.

To make your own square shaped seal, cut a bar of soap into six equal pieces. Each seal uses one piece of the soap. Use a toothpick to carve a design into the soap. You can make six different designs, one for each side of the soap. Remember that the design will come out opposite, so form letters your letters backward. Press your seal into play dough or salt dough.

To make a cylinder shaped seal, roll salt dough into a small cylinder then "carve" your design into the dough. Allow it to dry for a couple of days. Then you can use your seal to put your signature

Mesopotamia - Maps & Globes - Planets - Cave Paintings

on other wet "clay tablets" made of salt dough.

Salt Dough
1/2 c. salt
1 c. flour
½ c. water

Mix the flour and salt together. Add water and knead together. You can add food coloring or scents to make it more fun. You can also allow it to air dry for a hard, permanent model.

☺ ☺ ☺ **EXPLORATION: Nicknames**
Mesopotamia was a land that has been given many nicknames. It's called "The Land Between Two Rivers," "The Fertile Crescent," and "The Cradle of Western Civilization." Each nickname was symbolic and packed with meaning. Discuss what each of these nicknames means and how they describe the area. Over the centuries names have often reflected meaning. The Native American peoples were known for giving names that represented their personalities (like "Peaceful Heart" or "Fierce Warrior") What would be a fitting nickname for you? Why? You could also think of nicknames for your pet, car, home, city, or state. Write about your nicknames in your writer's notebook.

☺ ☺ **EXPLORATION: Mud Bricks**
Many ancient homes were made of simple mud bricks. You can make your own. Just save the grass clippings the next time you mow your lawn. Get a bucket and mix grass clippings, dirt, and enough water to turn the dirt into mud. Mix them all together and form them into 2 inch rectangular blocks. Set them out to dry in the sun. They will harden into perfect building blocks for creating a miniature home.

☺ ☺ ☺ **EXPLORATION: Inventions For Sale**
The Sumerians who lived in Mesopotamia were pretty smart folks. They invented a lot of really useful things that helped them in their everyday lives. The wheel, sailboats, frying pans, musical

Fabulous Fact
This statue is a worshiper. He was placed near the "Square Temple" at Tell Asmar to represent the perpetual prayers of his owner.

Just as the Mesopotamian people believed their gods actually inhabited the statues the people built for them, they believed humans could physically be present in a statue.

Photo by Rosemaniakos from Bejing, CC license, Wikimedia

Additional Layer
The type of homes we build depends on the climate we live in, as well as the natural building materials that are available.

How would it be to live in Arizona in an igloo? How about a dugout in Florida? Would a mud brick home work everywhere in the world?

MESOPOTAMIA - MAPS & GLOBES - PLANETS - CAVE PAINTINGS

Famous Folks

Enheduanna was the daughter of Sargon, who was king of the Akkadian Empire. She was also a high priestess. She encouraged her people to worship the goddess Inanna; she wrote hymns in honor of Inanna.

Enheduanna was the first writer to include her name with her writings. Because we know her by name, she is sometimes thought of as the first author and poet in the world. She told about her own life in the hymns she wrote as well.

This is the disk of Enheduanna. It shows her presiding over a purification ritual in the temple.

Fabulous Fact

The Epic of Gilgamesh has been found written on stone tablets, buried under the sand in Iraq. There are many thousands of stone tablets not yet translated and even more still buried.

---

instruments, kilns (used for baking bricks and pots), tools made of bronze, plows, make-up, and razors – all of these were invented by the ancient Sumerians. Choose one of these inventions and make an advertisement selling the new product. Have fun and use your imagination. You can do a printed ad or act out a commercial.

☺ ☺ ☺ **EXPLORATION: Mesopotamian Mural**

Make a wall mural of ancient Mesopotamia showing various aspects of their society. Religion could be represented by priests and a ziggurat. Inventions could be represented by sailboats, a plow, a wheel, frying pans, razors, harps, a kiln, and bronze tools. A king or clay tablets with laws written on them could represent government. You might draw it between two rivers to represent the geographic location. Finish the mural with people working and playing within their civilization.

EXPLANATION: Writing and Narration

Remember to follow up every unit section by writing about what was learned. Young kids can draw a picture and tell a narration. Older kids can write a paragraph to a page. By high school there should be complete essays. There is also a coloring sheet included with each history section for young kids who aren't ready for writing. You can keep all of your history writings together in order to create your own story of the history of our world.

☺ **EXPLORATION: Epic of Gilgamesh**

The Epic of Gilgamesh is the first epic story in the history of the

Mesopotamia - Maps & Globes - Planets - Cave Paintings

world. It is about a king named Gilgamesh who was a horrible despot until the wild man, Enkidu, becomes his friend. The two go off into the world having adventures together. But the gods get angry, so they kill Enkidu. Gilgamesh starts to fear his own death so he goes in search of Utnapishtim, an ancient man who is supposed to know the secret to eternal life. After many harrowing adventures he finds Utnapishtim, but the old man says he cannot help Gilgamesh. Eventually Gilgamesh returns to his city, reconciled to death. He sees the glory and beauty of his city and realizes that it will be his legacy, continuing on long after he has died. He becomes a good king.

The story is essentially about how a bad man became a good one. How does he do it? The answer to this question tells you a lot about the Mesopotamian world view. Read the *Epic of Gilgamesh* paying attention to the turning points in Gilgamesh's life. We recommend the version by Stephen Mitchell because it is the most readable. But, if the real thing is a bit much Sparknotes is an excellent resource for understanding Gilgamesh: http://www.sparknotes.com/lit/gilgamesh/

- Gilgamesh's transformation happens as he takes a journey. So as you read, draw a digram of the journey. It begins and ends in his city of Uruk. Gilgamesh comes full circle. So your basic path will be a circle, around which you will write the events of Gilgamesh's journey. What helped turn Gilgamesh from bad to good?

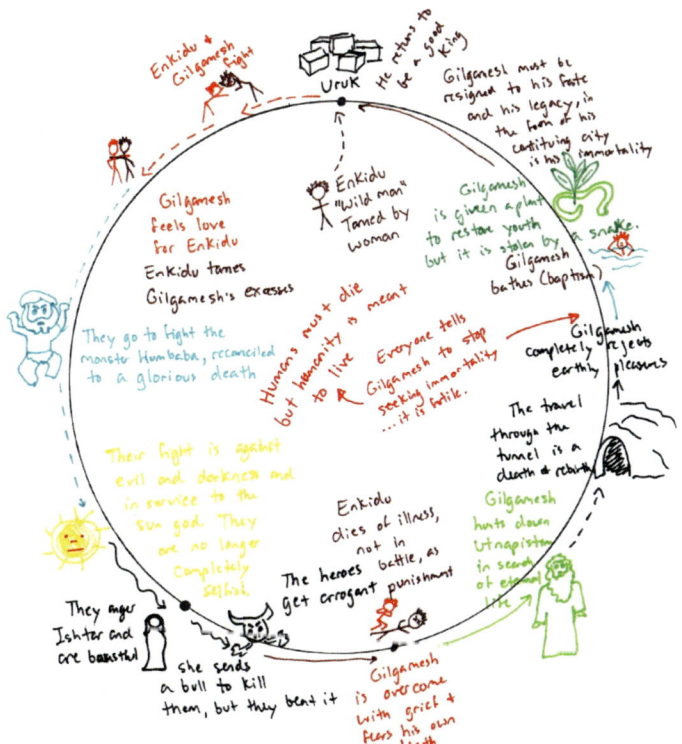

On the Web
Watch this video retelling of Gilgamesh for high school and up: https://www.youtube.com/watch?v=2pGhEu9elnA

On the Web
Watch Mr. Green humorously do a quick overview of Mesopotamia.

http://youtu.be/sohX-Px_XZ6Y

There is a naked "David" statue featured anachronistically and a drawing of people, you know, in bed. Preview.

Additional Layer
The nation next door to Sumer, in the east, was called Elam. It was pretty much as powerful and as advanced as Sumer, but no one ever talks about Elam.

Here is where Elam is situated along the eastern shore of the Persian Gulf.

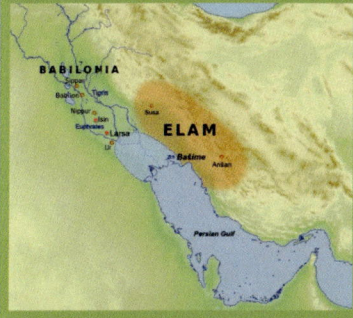

You can read up on it a bit at Wikipedia or in another encyclopedia.

MESOPOTAMIA - MAPS & GLOBES - PLANETS - CAVE PAINTINGS

GEOGRAPHY: MAPS & GLOBES

Teaching Tip

Look through an atlas with your child. It would be a good idea to purchase a student atlas to use throughout their school years. Point out how the atlas is organized and find the key or legend on several maps.

Additional Layer

An atlas is a book of maps. There were two mythical figures named Atlas that have been associated with books of maps. The first was King Atlas who supposedly made the first celestial globe.

The second was a Greek mythological figure who was punished by Zeus and told he would forever have to hold the weight of the heavens on his back.

He was said to live in the west and the Atlas mountains and Atlantic Ocean were both named after him.

Globes are the most accurate models of the earth, but they have their drawbacks too. They're really tough to get into your glove compartment, they are too small to show the streets in your town or even the major highways in your country, and they're bulky to store. Globes are fascinating to search and explore though. Take time to just look, touch, spin it, and turn it upside down.

A map is a flat drawing that represents a real place on earth. Almost everybody enjoys looking at a good map. They're not only tools, but they're also often art. The oldest maps we know of are not terribly accurate geographically speaking. They would often be roughly correct in their placement of highways and cities, but they also included lots of storytelling or embellishment. Monsters would be drawn along the margins or deep treacherous valleys would be exaggerated to warn people off. The unknown would be speculated about, but from the beginning, symbols have been used on maps to represent real things. On modern maps the symbols are explained in a key. It's like a secret code, with the translation given so anyone who wants to can read it.

Ancient maps didn't show the whole earth or even a very large portion of it. Accurate maps of the whole world have only been produced in the last hundred years. Until we could actually see the earth from above, first from balloons and airplanes, and then from satellites in space, we couldn't draw a perfect picture of what was below. Drawing the earth as it really is is still challenging

MESOPOTAMIA - MAPS & GLOBES - PLANETS - CAVE PAINTINGS

though, because maps are flat and the earth is not. Cartographers, or map makers, use different projections, or methods of squishing a round earth onto a flat piece of paper to make maps as accurate as possible. The projection they use depends on what the map is used for. The three kinds of projections are cylindrical, azimuthal, and conic.

☺ ☺ ☻ EXPLORATION: Getting To Know The Globe

Using a globe, identify:

- Land and oceans
- Hemispheres: north, south, west, east
- Poles
- Equator, arctic circles, tropic circles
- Your location on the globe

For older students:

- Analemma: figure 8 shape that shows the procession of the sun in relation to earth
- International date line
- 0 degree line of longitude
- Compass rose
- Key or legend
- Scale
- Magnetic north and magnetic south poles

☺ ☺ EXPLORATION: Draw Your Own Globe

Inflate a round balloon, one for each child and one for the teacher. White or light blue colored balloons will work best. Give everyone a set of markers in the basic colors. If you'd like the balloon to stand up an adult can cut an X in a piece of flat cardboard with a knife and pull the tied spout of the balloon through the X so the balloon will stay in place on the cardboard.

As a group you are going to make a globe of your own.

1. Draw the continents (it's okay if they're pretty rough).
2. Label continents and oceans.
3. Draw a mark for the north pole and one for the south pole.
4. Draw the equator.
5. Draw the Prime Meridian.
6. Add other marks such as the Tropic of Cancer and the Tropic of Capricorn, the arctic circles, the international dateline, and so on.
7. Find where your city is and mark it with a big star.

Additional Layer

The prefixes hemi, demi, and semi all mean half, but are used in different ways.

Hemi means one side, like a hemisphere on one side of the globe.

Demi means less (or almost, but not quite); demi-millionaire means almost a millionaire.

Semi means partly, as in semi-civilized, meaning only partly civilized.

On the Web

Watch a simple video "Maps and Globes": https://www.youtube.com/watch?v=phX-4cZFen_0&t

Additional Layer

No one knows for sure how Shakespeare's The Globe Theater got its name. It may have been because of the globe-like shape, or perhaps it was tied into its motto: *Totus mundus agit historium* ("the whole world is a playhouse").

In Shakespeare's *As You Like It*, he reworded it a bit to become the famous "All the world's a stage."

Mesopotamia - Maps & Globes - Planets - Cave Paintings

Additional Layer

Globes themselves can be works of art. Check out these globes:

- Unisphere globe in New York City
- Mappariam at the Mary Baker Eddy Library in Boston, Massachussetts
- Eartha in Yarmouth, Maine.

Photo of Eartha by John Phelan, CC license, Wikimedia

Additional Layer

Combine art and geography with *Where in the World? Around the Globe in 13 Works of Art* by Bob Raczk.

As you read about art from different places in the world, find the locations on your globe.

Fabulous Fact

All the continents except Europe begin with an "A".

☺ ☺ EXPLORATION: Foam Globe

Make a globe out of a small foam craft ball. Paint the green continents and blue oceans. Use your earth later to add to your planets craft in the science section of this unit.

☺ ☺ ☺ EXPLORATION: Paper Maché Globe

Blow up a balloon. If you don't blow it up too much it will have a more rounded shape. Make paper maché paste (1 c. boiling water, 1 c. flour, mixed well) and tear or cut newspapers into long strips. Dip the paper into the paste and cover the whole balloon with the papers, criss-crossing each other. The more layers of paper you put on, the stronger it will be. Around three layers is about right. Let it dry for a couple of days.

Spray paint the whole globe blue. Next, cut out the continents from a map of the world and glue onto your globe. You can use a blank outline map and color it ahead of time, marking where you live. You can also use a color map and just glue the continents on. If you'd like, you can paint the continents on instead of pasting them. As a challenge for older kids see if they can paint the continents without looking at a map. How well do they know the globe?

☺ ☺ ☺ EXPLORATION: Globe Trotter

Spin the globe and put your finger somewhere on it to stop it (Try to hit land!). Now look up some information about the spot you landed on. Where could you stay? What kinds of foods will you find there? Are you more likely to find big cities full of people, small villages, or animal habitats? What's the weather like? What will you need to pack? Include the information in a travel brochure. You can find a printable template for a travel brochure at www.layers-of-learning.com/travel-brochure and at the end of this unit.

☺ ☺ EXPLORATION: ABC's Around The Globe Game

The first person chooses a place on the globe that starts with A, then you find that place. The second person thinks of a place that starts with B, and you find that spot, the third person thinks of a place that starts with C, and you find that spot, and so on all the way through the alphabet.

You can play this as a competition where the person who can't think of a place that begins with that letter is out. Keep going around and around the alphabet, never repeating a place, until one winner is left. Or you can play as a cooperative game, where the group thinks or searches for places with each letter of the alphabet.

Mesopotamia - Maps & Globes - Planets - Cave Paintings

😊 😊 **EXPERIMENT: Analemma**

On most globes you'll find a funny figure 8 shape printed, usually somewhere in the Pacific Ocean. It's called an analemma. As the earth orbits the sun in its elliptical path it gets closer, then further away, causing the speed of the earth to change slightly. The speed change makes the sun move its position at midday relative to the surface of the earth. The earth's tilt also causes the sun to move north and then south, relative to the earth's surface.

You can test this out by placing a large upright stake in a permanent position outside. Every day for a year mark the position of the end of the shadow at exactly the same time of day (remember to ignore daylight savings time). At the end of a year you will have marked out a figure 8 pattern.

😊 😊 😊 **EXPLORATION: Globes Versus Maps**

Create a chart and list the advantages and disadvantages of using globes versus maps. Your chart may start like this. See how much you can add to it.

Globes Versus Maps	Advantages	Disadvantages
Globes	Really accurate because it has the right shape.	Can't find my way around town using one!
Maps	Easy to fold up and store.	Doesn't have the right shape to reflect the earth.

😊 **EXPLORATION: Hemispheres**

The earth can be divided into fractions, in our imaginations anyway. Hemi means "half" so "hemisphere" is half of a sphere. Use apples or oranges to show how a sphere can be divided in half two ways. The stem and scar on the opposite side can represent the poles. Cut the first piece of fruit in half from pole to pole. This divides it into east and west hemispheres. Show where the east and west hemispheres are on a globe. Now take a second piece of fruit and cut it along the "equator." This represents the north and south hemispheres. Point out the mark on the globe for the equator and where the north and south hemispheres are.

😊 😊 **EXPLORATION: Where in the Solar System?**

Show the kids a picture of the solar system and point out where the earth is. Name each planet and talk about where the earth is located. Which planets are nearest to earth? Point out the Moon.

Teaching Tip

Reading a map requires abstract thinking, which kids typically develop between ages 7 and 9. Most younger kids won't yet understand that a map represents a real place, but they can still be introduced to maps and globes.

Fabulous Fact

You can see a figure eight shaped analemma on this globe. Try to find it on a globe of your own

Additional Layer

Compare what a cartographer's job would have been 50 years ago to what it would be like today. Consider the technology that currently exists.

Additional Layer

We keep time by the sun, moon, and stars, and the times are determined by the position and location and other features of earth in space. Make a sundial.

Mesopotamia - Maps & Globes - Planets - Cave Paintings

Additional Layer
The early models of the earth, sun, moon, and stars were called armillary spheres. They were models made to explain different theories about the revolution of the planets and their relationship to one another. Look some up online.

Famous Folks
Ptolemy was an early geography, astronomer, and poet. He wrote *Geographia*, in which he compiled all that was known of the geography of the world in his day.

His maps weren't necessarily accurate, but it was more complete than the previous maps that had been created.

Ptolemy's world map

How far from the sun is earth? How long does it take to travel around the sun? Why does the earth have seasons? What makes day and night? You can simply discuss these things or you can assign a report on a particular aspect of earth in space.

☻ EXPLORATION: Where I Live
Make a book showing where you live. On each page you will move from your most exact location to a more general one. The first page should be about your house, then your city, then your state or province, then your country, then your continent, then your planet, then your solar system. You can find a printable template to get you started at the end of this unit.

Cut the pages on the dotted line. Arrange the sheets from shortest to tallest. Choose between using the "state" or the "province" page. Have your child illustrate each page, filling them with color. This is a big project for little kids. You may want to spend an entire week or more on it, doing a little at a time and talking about it as you go.

☻ EXPLORATION: Continents & Oceans
Begin to memorize the continents. Young kids who are just being introduced to the world will need lots of practice before they know the major continents and oceans. Some books and other resources have started naming Oceania as a continent in place of Australia and in that way including all the South Pacific Islands

20

MESOPOTAMIA - MAPS & GLOBES - PLANETS - CAVE PAINTINGS

and Australia as one geographical region. Name it the way you like. Pick from this list of ways to practice and do a short activity two or three times a week until they've got it.

- Put a world map up on the wall and point to the continents and oceans while the kids name them, or name them and have the kids point them out.
- Print out blank world maps, have the kids color the continents, a different color for each continent, color the oceans blue, then cut it apart to make a puzzle. (Print the map out on card stock to make a sturdier puzzle or glue your paper to cereal box cardboard before cutting apart.
- Purchase a world map puzzle to practice with.
- Pre-cut the continents from a blank outline map. Have the kids place the continents in the correct places.
- On a blank outline map of the world have the kids paste the pre-printed continent names. You can also write them in yellow highlighter and have them trace the names if you want them to practice handwriting a bit.
- Play an online game to practice like "Globe Rider" at Funschool.kaboose.com or sheppardsoftware.com. Search for "continents geography games" for many more.
- Play pin the compass rose on the continents. Give each child a printed compass rose, or have them draw one. Write their name on it. Blindfold them in turn and have them try to pin (or tape) their compass rose to the continent or ocean you name on a world map on the wall. You can do this over and over until you've named several or all of them.
- Purchase a Geography Music CD, like *Geography Songs* by Larry and Kathy Troxel. Includes a song for the continents and oceans and many more for specific countries and continents. Listen to the target song several times in a row while pointing to the continents. You can also find songs on You Tube or download just the "Continents" song from Geography Songs.
- Draw a really big map of the world on an outdoor concrete surface with chalk and have the kids move to the continent or ocean you call out.
- Quiz the kids by having them follow fun directions to color the map, like draw a whale in the Atlantic Ocean, color Europe green, draw the south pole on Antarctica, draw a sailing ship in the Pacific Ocean, draw the Great Wall of China in Asia, draw a hamburger in North America, put an orange X on Australia, and so on.
- Need LOTS of easy to prepare practice? Buy an inexpensive workbook dedicated to the continents and oceans like The Continents by Jeanne Cheyenne.

Teaching Tip

First Atlas from DK is great for the youngest kids.

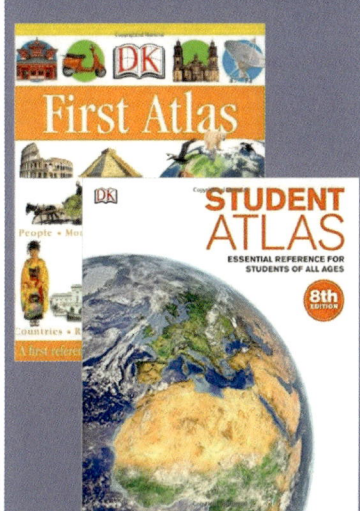

Middle and high school kids should like the *Student Atlas* from DK.

But visit your local library and browse through several of their student atlases to see what you like before you buy. The atlas you pick should appeal to your child.

Writer's Workshop

Make an acrostic poem about a globe. Write the word globe down the left hand side of the paper. Look at the globe and try to find places on it that begin with each letter in the word globe.

Georgia
Laos
Oceania
Beliz
Equator

Mesopotamia - Maps & Globes - Planets - Cave Paintings

Teaching Tip
For little ones, gather some small toys like a doll house and dolls, or little cars. Explain that they aren't really houses, people, and vehicles; they are models that are much smaller than the real thing. They represent what these things are like in real life. A globe is just a small version of our planet earth. It's much littler, but shows what our big planet earth looks like.

Additional Layer
This is a great time to cover or review 3-dimensional shapes like spheres, cubes, prisms, cones, pyramids, and cylinders. Point out that globe is a sphere.

On the Web
Enchanted Learning has several map reading activities including work with map legends, compass rose, map reading and so on:

www.enchantedlearning.com/geography/mapreading/

Some of these topics are covered in this unit, some will be covered in the next several units in Layers of Learning.

☺ ☻ EXPLORATION: So You Think You Know the Continents?
The continents, countries, oceans, and world map as a whole are nearly always portrayed from the same orientation, with north at the top. But they don't have to be; that's just convention. Cut out continent and ocean shapes from a blank world map and present them to the kids upside down or sideways, or even at an angle and ask them if they know where in the world this is. Show them views of the north and south pole as seen straight on, instead of the widely distorted view we usually see. Have them take a pre-quiz. Then explain what you did and have them take a post-quiz. Did they improve?

☺ ☻ ☻ EXPLORATION: My Town, U.S.A.
Look up a map of your state or town. Point out the legend on the map. What symbols are shown? Help your child find the symbols on the map as well. What colors are shown? Do different colors represent different things? For example, on many city maps a green space will represent a park. Highways might be drawn in red while residential streets are black.

☺ ☻ ☻ EXPLORATION: Google Maps
To show how maps are pictures of real places go online and look up your city or your neighborhood on Google Maps. There will be an actual aerial view of your neighborhood from space and then you can click on the map view and see what it looks like as a picture. See if you can find your house.

22

MESOPOTAMIA - MAPS & GLOBES - PLANETS - CAVE PAINTINGS

☺ ☻ **EXPLORATION: My Own Map**
Draw a map of your house and yard (either inside or outside). Use symbols and a key to represent different things. How will you represent windows and doors? How will you represent a bedroom or child's play area?

☺ ☻ **EXPLORATION: Pirates and Wizards and Fairies, Oh My!**
Draw a map of an imaginary place like a pirate island or a magical kingdom. Use a key to show important features like roads, trails, buried treasure, a fort, a place of danger, a town and so on.

☺ ☻ **EXPERIMENT: A Mapmaker's Troubles**
Carefully peel an orange so that the peel is in as few pieces as possible. Now try to flatten the orange peel into one smooth sheet. Now you know the problems makers of flat maps have. If you are mapping a small area (like one city) it's not so bad, but if you want to do a whole continent or the whole earth you have problems getting everything to fit without stretching some parts and squishing others.

☺ ☻ **EXPLORATION: Map Projections**
The three major types of map projections are conical, cylindrical, and azimuthal. To demonstrate how each of these works, get a sphere (like a ball or an orange) and a sheet of paper.

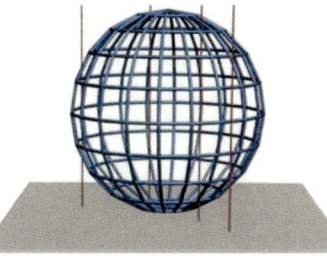

This shows the conical, cylindrical, and azimuthal projections. Image by Traroth, CC license, Wikimedia.

To show a conical projection, make your paper into a cone shape and place over the ball with the sides of the cone touching around the circumference, like the ball is wearing a dunce cap. The least amount of distortion is at the bottom edge of the paper, where it touches the ball. As you move further up the distortion increases. You are left with a fan shaped map. This type of map is useful for showing a single country from the globe.

For the cylindrical projection, place the paper around the ball in a cylinder, then imagine the surface of the ball projected onto the cylinder, like a mirror. The area near the center or "equator" of

---

Memorization Station

Continents
- North America
- South America
- Asia
- Europe
- Africa
- Australia
- Antarctica

Oceans
- Pacific
- Atlantic
- Arctic
- Antarctic (Southern)
- Indian

Practice these until you have them down. For young kids new to the continents and oceans this may take many tiny memorizing sessions.

At the end of this unit there is a colored printable of the continents for you to use as you wish. You can label it, cut it apart, cover it with contact paper or laminate it and quiz over it. Post it near the dinner table so you remember to review.

Make it tougher for older kids by expecting them to know seas and subcontinents as well. Make it into a game for motivation.

23

Mesopotamia - Maps & Globes - Planets - Cave Paintings

On the Web
"Why all world maps are wrong" is a good video that explains why flat maps are never right: https://www.youtube.com/watch?v=kIID5F-Di2JQ

On the Web
For a much more detailed look at specific projections visit: https://egsc.usgs.gov/isb//pubs/MapProjections/projections.html

Fabulous Fact
Besides map projections being classified based on their geometry they can be classed according to their purpose:
- Preserving direction
- Preserving area
- Preserving shape
- Preserving distance
- Preserving shortest route

Famous Folks
In 1569 Gerard Mercator invented a new way of drawing maps that made navigation much easier.

the ball will be accurate, a perfect image, but the areas further from the "equator", toward the poles will become more and more stretched out. On most flat maps of the earth, Greenland is enormously stretched out. Compare the size of Greenland on a globe to its size on a flat map. The popular Mercator projection is a cylindrical projection as is the Robinson projection, though it is modified to squish the tops and bottoms of the map to make the scale closer to true.

An azimuthal projection picks one point on the globe to be the central point from which the map stretches out. Place the flat paper against one side of the ball and imagine the ball projected onto the paper. The center point will have the least distortion and the further from that central point you get, the more stretched out the map will be. This type of map is useless for a picture of the whole globe, since at least one half can't be seen at all. But it can be useful for a continent size map. This type of map is used most often to show the poles.

The front of your child's student atlas should have more information and pictures of various map projections. The USGS has a good explanation of several of the most common types of map projections at www.egsc.usgs.gov/isb/pubs/MapProjections/projections.html.

EXPLANATION: Organizing a Study Space

A dedicated study space is not a necessity. What you do need is a place you regularly study and storage space for school supplies.

You can study at your dining table, in the living room, or at desks

MESOPOTAMIA - MAPS & GLOBES - PLANETS - CAVE PAINTINGS

in a school room. The study space should be kept clear so you have room when it comes to school time. We have also found that it's really nice to have some sort of a "board" to write things on. It can be a chalkboard or white board on the wall or it can just be a hand held one. You can also use a window and a wet erase marker.

To store your supplies a dresser, a set of cupboards, a kitchen cabinet, or a bookshelf with bins will be needed. We admit to having a ton of school supplies, but you can actually store everything you need in one plastic tub per child or on one shelf if you are willing to cut out the clutter and buy art and science supplies only as you need them.

The more organized and neat you can keep your study area, the less stress you will feel in your homeschool. Achieve this by training the children to pick up after themselves and establishing a routine of picking up everyday after school.

☺ ☺ ☺ EXPLORATION: Make Your Own Atlas

Begin making your own atlas. You can include some of the maps you made in this unit and any others you'd like. Make maps of places you'd like to travel and places you've been. Make a map showing your route to your piano lesson or soccer practice. Make a treasure map of your neighborhood and hide a treasure. Fill your atlas with all kinds of maps. Create a nice cover design and compile it into a book. You can use a three ring binder if you want to continually add to it, or have it bound at a copy center. Maps truly can be works of art so take time and do superb work.

Explanation

Mostly, I do not have the school room (or the house) of my dreams, but you never know about the future. I like to be prepared with a plan, for just in case some long lost and very rich relative dies and leaves me a fortune. Hey, it could happen.

One of my favorite things over the years has been to have a design notebook for house decorating and building ideas.

Keep a list of the essentials you want/need for school spaces. And then search around for good deals at thrift stores, discount stores and so on. Be patient and save up for what you really want instead of settling for something that will "do" for now.

Library List

The "Castle Glower" series, by Jessica Day George, would be a fun read aloud while learning about maps. The story includes a magical castle with moving hallways and disappearing rooms. The young princess in the tale decides to make an atlas of the castle so the people who live there can find their way around.

MESOPOTAMIA - MAPS & GLOBES - PLANETS - CAVE PAINTINGS

SCIENCE: PLANETS

Teaching Tip
During this unit you'll be learning about a lot of concepts. Here are a few things to consider covering:
- The solar system and our planets
- The elliptical orbit of planets around our sun
- Asteroid belt
- Comets and meteors
- Planets surround other stars too
- Galaxies and the Universe
- Types of Galaxies (spiral, elliptical, and irregular)

Fabulous Fact
There's a good explanation for the location of the asteroid belt. Jupiter's huge size gives it a huge gravitational pull. The proximity of the asteroids to Jupiter's gravity likely kept that group of asteroids from continuing to form with the other planets.

Additional Layer
Learning a foreign language? Learn the names of the planets in the language you are studying.

Huge balls of rock, ice, magma, and gases are all hurling around an immense ball of heat, our sun. Planets are suspended in an unknown substance of something or nothing; no one is quite sure which. Celestial bodies are all falling toward each other, but seldom colliding. Small bits of dust are flaming into death. Big bits of ice and rock are streaming across the heavens, swirling, rocking, and whipping through space in seeming abandon, but actually all in a very orderly and predictable way. This is our solar system.

Our solar system seems huge to us, yet it's only a speck in the galaxy, and our galaxy is only a speck inside the universe. There is much we are still learning about space and all that's out there, but we do know a great deal about our own solar system. A solar system is just a star and its orbiting planets. Our Sun is our star. A planet is basically a big round thing that orbits around a star, everybody knows that, but scientists like specifics, so the official definition is currently (because you never know when they'll change it again) that a planet is an object orbiting the Sun, has enough mass to make it round, and has cleared its path of other celestial bodies. So Pluto, which used to be considered a planet, isn't anymore because its path contains asteroids and stuff. The problem see, is that scientists keep discovering bodies orbiting the Sun that are about as big or even bigger than Pluto, like some of the asteroids in the asteroid belt and other bodies way out near Neptune. The scientists decided they had to draw the line somewhere, so they drew it so that it cut Pluto off.

MESOPOTAMIA - MAPS & GLOBES - PLANETS - CAVE PAINTINGS

There are eight planets in our solar system: Mercury, Venus, Earth, Mars, Jupiter, Saturn, Uranus, and Neptune. There are other planets in other solar systems as well; we call these extra-solar planets, or exoplanets. We've never actually seen most of them, but we've noticed that they create "wobbles" (or small dips in brightness) for their star. NASA's Kepler Space Telescope is designed to find Earth-size planets outside of our solar system, and is doing just that. More and more we are able to see exoplanets in other solar systems since first using the Kepler in 2010. It's likely that nearly every star has many planets orbiting it, just like our Sun does.

☺ ● **EXPLORATION: Solar System Model**
Get various sized foam balls from a craft store. You'll need five relatively small, three large, one extra large and one huge (the sun). Paint them to look like each planet. Hang them from strings from your ceiling in order of orbit around the sun. Quiz the kids over the names and order of the planets from time to time over the next couple of weeks.

☺ ● **EXPLORATION: Planet Report**
Make a poster or write a report featuring a particular planet. Include location in the solar system, atmosphere, structure of the planet, size compared to earth, three or four interesting facts, who discovered it and when, and a printed picture or your child's illustration of the planet. Older kids should have more complicated and involved reports.

Teaching Tip

For the most part the experiments you'll find in Layers of Learning are pre-digested. We give you the procedure, expected outcome, and lesson to learn. They therefore don't really qualify as "experiments" at all. In a real experiment, you would design the procedure and find your own conclusions.

But you can still help kids understand how real scientists work, by asking them lots of questions and getting their ideas before you give them the answers.

And you can explain the scientific method and have them record their process. Use the printable *Scientific Method Experiment Write-up* found at www.layers-of-learning.com/a-simple-introduction-to-the-scientific-method/.

Additional Layer

This is the astronomical symbol for Uranus. It is a globe surmounted by the letter "h" for Herschel, the discoverer of Uranus. All the major bodies in the solar system have a symbol.

27

Mesopotamia - Maps & Globes - Planets - Cave Paintings

Writer's Workshop

Imagine blasting off in a spaceship and landing on a new, undiscovered planet! What is it like there? Are there oceans, forests, lakes, deserts, or ice? Do the aliens look like people from earth? So far we've never found a planet that can sustain life like earth can, so use your imagination and write about what you might find. Don't forget to name your new planet!

Teaching Tip

Each day start out your lesson with a review of past learning. Turn it into a game with a chance to win points that go toward something fun. Rehearsing information over and over is how we really learn.

Fabulous Fact

Voyager 2 flew past Neptune and shot photos of the surface on August 16 and 17, 1989. The great dark spot on the surface is no longer there.

EXPERIMENT: Mercury is Too Hot

Mercury is much closer to the sun than the earth. Being nearer to the sun means it gets really hot on Mercury, but it can also cool off to temperatures far below those of Earth, because Mercury has no atmosphere. Without an atmosphere, or a blanket of air, there is nothing to hold the heat in. To see how a planet closer to the sun gets much hotter try this experiment:

1. Place a desk lamp so it shines at an angle onto a smooth surface, like a counter top.
2. Place two thermometers, one very close to the lamp, in the beam and one several inches further away, but still in the beam.
3. Check the temperature on both thermometers every minute for the next ten minutes.

Before you begin, form a hypothesis of what you think will happen. Write it at the top of a paper. Make a table showing your data and then write your results and what you conclude being closer to a heat source does to temperature.

EXPERIMENT: Venus, The Evening Star

Venus is the easiest planet to spot. Keep an eye on the sky just before sunrise or just after sunset, while there is light in the sky, but the sun is not over the horizon. If you see a bright star in the light sky near the sun, that's Venus. They call it the morning and the evening star.

To see why you can see it only in the morning or the evening near the sun, try this experiment:

1. Have one person hold an uncovered light bulb to represent the sun. They should stand in the center of the room.
2. Have another person hold a very small ball to represent Venus. They should stand a few feet from the sun.
3. A third person should then hold another small ball to represent the earth. They should stand several feet further from the sun, directly in line with the sun and Venus. (The greater the distance between Venus and Earth the better, but the size of Earth's orbit must be constrained by the size of the room.)
4. Darken the room so the only light comes from the sun.
5. Now you are going to simulate the orbit of the planets around the sun. The two planets should move about the same speed. Venus will travel around the sun more quickly though because it has less distance to travel.
6. Every now and then say "freeze." The planets will stop their orbit. Ask the group if they were standing on earth could they

see Venus and where would it be in the sky?

Venus cannot be seen if it is either on the opposite side of the sun from the earth or if it is directly in line with the sun. Venus will never rise in the middle of the night because it is between us and the sun. It must always be near the sun.

😊 😊 😊 **EXPERIMENT: Earth, The Goldilocks Planet**
Earth is sometimes called the Goldilocks planet because conditions are just right for life – not too hot, not too cold, not too much gravity, not too little, not too long a year, not too short; you get the idea. One of the keys to that is Earth's atmosphere. An atmosphere is very important. If you don't have one at all (like Mercury) you go through wild temperature swings from way too hot in the day to way too cold at night. If you have too much atmosphere (like Venus) you stay terribly hot all the time and the pressure of all that stuff in the air is crushing as well. To see how atmosphere acts to regulate heat, try this experiment:

1. Get two identical containers, like plastic dishes or glass jars.
2. Place thermometers inside, arranging them so you'll be able to see the temperatures.
3. Place plastic wrap over the top of one of the containers and secure with a rubber band.
4. Place the containers in the sun.
5. Take note of the temperature every ten minutes for the next 30 min to an hour.
6. Remove the containers into the shade or indoors.
7. Record the temperature again for the next 30 minutes to an hour.

What did you notice about the temperature of the two dishes when they were in the sun? What about when they were in the shade? What happens if you add a third dish which has colored plastic wrap instead of clear?

In this experiment the plastic wrap represents the atmosphere of a planet. The atmosphere helps collect and hold heat, but it can also shield a planet from radiation and some heat as well (like the colored plastic wrap). At night the Earth's temperature drops, but only a very little bit, because the atmosphere holds in the heat.

😊 😊 **EXPERIMENT: The Regressive Orbit of Mars**
Mars moves in a regressive pattern, appearing as though it's moving backward, but actually it is just slower than earth.

To witness how a regressive orbit works, go get two toy cars and a block. Move the cars along a table in the same direction, with the

On the Web

The three major types of galaxies are spiral, elliptical and irregular. Their names describe their shapes. Spiral galaxies look like spirals, ellipticals look like elongated circles and irregulars are sort of blobs.

You can see amazing pictures of all three types at Hubblesite.org.

This is a montage of many differnt galaxies that have been photographed.

Additional Layer

In ancient times the Greeks and Romans named the planets they could see after their gods and goddesses.

Astronomers since then have kept up the tradition. The Milky Way gets its name from an old Greek myth that milk was splashed from the breast of Juno, mother of Hercules.

Read more about this myth.

Mesopotamia - Maps & Globes - Planets - Cave Paintings

Additional Layer

Find out more about aurora borealis and aurora australis. You may want to check out You Tube to see some videos if you haven't witnessed this phenomena in person.

Famous Folks

Johannes Kepler was a German astronomer and mathematician. He was one of the most important scientists in the early study of astronomy. He wrote the 3 laws of planetary motion and also described how the moon influenced the tides.

He was the first one to unite physics and astronomy.

block behind them in the background. Move one car faster than the other.

At first the block is in front of both cars, but after a moment, a passenger in the first car would have to look backward to see the block. From the point of view of the faster car it looks like the slower car is moving backward, but it's not. It's just slower. Mars moves slower around the sun than earth does, so for part of the time it looks like Mars is moving backward.

☺ ☻ **EXPERIMENT: Asteroid Belt Physics**

Between Mars and Jupiter there is a ring of micro planets, also known as asteroids. They are rocky bits that scientists think are left over from the formation of the planets. They just didn't have enough mass to form into a planet of their own. Some of them are tiny pebbles and others are as big across as the state of Texas. So why do they stay in orbit instead of falling toward the greatest gravity, the sun?

1. You need a round, straight sided pan, like a cake or pie pan or a round casserole dish. You also need a marble and some

Mesopotamia - Maps & Globes - Planets - Cave Paintings

construction paper.
2. Cut the sheet of construction paper so it fits exactly in the bottom of the dish. Place the paper inside.
3. Roll the marble around the inside edge of the pan and see how long it will go.
4. Now remove the paper and get the marble started around again. Now how long did it go?

When you reduce the friction (by removing the paper), the marble spun for longer inside the pan. When the planets and the asteroids began to spin around the sun they had enough velocity to cause them to orbit. There is no friction in space and so they will never slow down.

😊 😊 EXPERIMENT: Jupiter – The Stormy Planet

One of the things that causes weather is the rotation of a planet. Jupiter rotates fast and this causes some wild weather on this planet made mostly of gas. The Great Red Spot (that's its official name, though we're sure you can think of better names) is the center of a permanent storm on Jupiter. To see how the Great Red Spot is created by swirling winds try this:

1. Fill a glass jar three quarters full of water.
2. Drop some tea leaves, coffee grounds, or bouillon granules into the water. (It doesn't really matter what you drop in as long as it has small particles and sinks in water.)
3. Stir rapidly with a spoon until you make a swirling whirlpool.

The swirling whirlpool is exactly the same sort of force that creates hurricanes on Earth and in the much more violent atmosphere of Jupiter creates a permanent storm in the Great Red Spot.

😊 😊 EXPERIMENT: Saturn's Rings

Saturn's Rings are made of bits of ice and dust, most of them very tiny. If it's so small, why can we see the debris so well from Earth? Try this:

1. You need a flashlight, baby powder or cornstarch, and a dark room.
2. Sprinkle some baby powder into the air. Pushing on the sides of the container will make a nice puff of powder into the air.
3. Point the flashlight at the particles.
4. You can see them really well because the light shines and reflects on them. If the room was light you wouldn't notice them much, but against the dark background they make a pretty show, just like Saturn's rings.

Memorization Station

Memorize the planets and their order. Don't forget to include the asteroid belt. Older kids can memorize some of the larger moons as well.

This is a montage of Jupiter and its four largest moons: Io, Callisto, Europa, and Ganymede.

Additional Layer

Read the Sparknotes explanation of the importance of the changes in astronomy during the scientific revolution. www.sparknotes.com/history/european/scientificrevolution/section2.rhtml

Deep Thoughts

Watch this "Copernicus - Mini Biography": https://www.youtube.com/watch?v=Mop6NK-ANE08

Mesopotamia - Maps & Globes - Planets - Cave Paintings

Fabulous Fact

The Kepler Space Telescope, located in orbit around Earth, has the mission of searching for planets outside our solar system. It primarily uses the transit method to detect these planets. The transit method searches for the shadow of a planet, a tiny black dot, and watches for the moment when it crosses a distant star.

The telescope can detect the tiny dip in brightness coming from the star caused by the shadow of the planet crossing it.

On the Web

Check out www.nineplanets.org to learn about the history, mythology, and scientific knowledge of all the planets and other things in our solar system.

And this site: www.kidsastronomy.com/solar_system.htm is excellent for younger kids.

EXPERIMENT: Uranus is Spinning Sideways!

Uranus spins on its side when compared to the other planets. All the planets spin, because if they didn't they wouldn't be planets; they'd be big, erratic wrecking balls of the solar system. The spin actually keeps them on an even keel.

Try this:

1. Get a paper plate, heavier paper ones work best. Place four paper clips around the rim of the plate equidistant from one another so they quarter the plate. Attach a string in the exact center of the plate.
2. Holding onto the string, swing the plate in front of you from left to right.
3. Now give the plate a spin as you swing it.

Spinning the plate keeps it from flopping around willy nilly. Any erratic flipping around in a planet would create forces that would throw it off its orbit and we'd have cosmic bumper cars instead of nice dependable orbits.

EXPERIMENT: Neptune's Elliptical Orbit

The orbits of the planets around the sun aren't round; they're elliptical, an oval shape. Neptune is 4.46 billion kilometers from the sun at its closest point and 4.54 billion kilometers from the sun at its furthest point. The point when a planet is at its closest is called the perihelion and the point when a planet is furthest from the sun is called the aphelion.

1. To show what an elliptical orbit of a planet looks like you'll need a string 12 inches long and a large sheet of paper placed over a thick piece of cardboard.
2. Place two tacks in the center of the paper about 1 inch apart and with the ends of the string being held down by the tacks. Tie knots in the ends of the string for the tacks to go through so it will hold.
3. Now place a pencil in the loop of the string and, holding the string taut, draw a complete oval around the tacks.

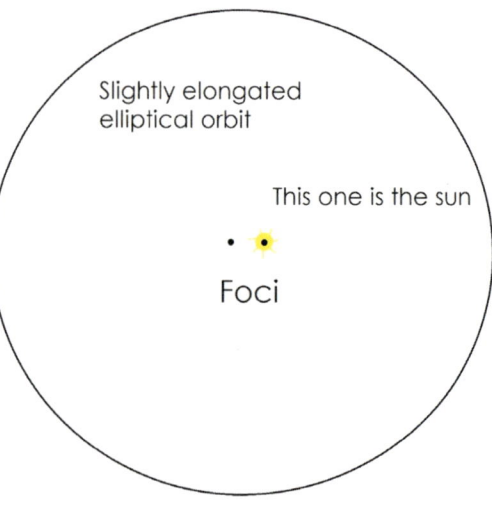

MESOPOTAMIA - MAPS & GLOBES - PLANETS - CAVE PAINTINGS

The tacks represent the foci of the ellipse. In the solar system the sun is one focus, and another point in space is the other focus. Sometimes the elliptical orbits of planets are shown very elongated, but they are actually pretty close to being circular, just a little off. They're not perfectly circular because the sun is not the only source of gravitation in the solar system. Other planets and even nearby solar systems can throw off the balance slightly.

😊 😊 😊 EXPEDITION: Planetarium

Find out if there's a planetarium near you. Visit it to see models of the planets and find out more facts about each one.

😊 EXPERIMENT: Shining Planets

Why do planets shine when we know they don't give off light like a star? Go get a flashlight and a ball, and take them to a very dark room. Shine the flashlight on the surface of the ball. You can see the ball because the light is bouncing off the ball; in other words, it is reflecting. Planets and moons don't make light of their own; they just reflect light from the sun.

😊 😊 EXPLORATION: Map of the Milky Way

The Milky Way, our galaxy, is a spiral galaxy. On dark construction paper (dark blue, purple or black) make long curving glue lines from a central point. Use a picture of the milky way galaxy to get the basic shape. Then cover the glue with glitter to represent the arms of the milky way galaxy. Draw an arrow to a point on one of the arms and write "solar system."

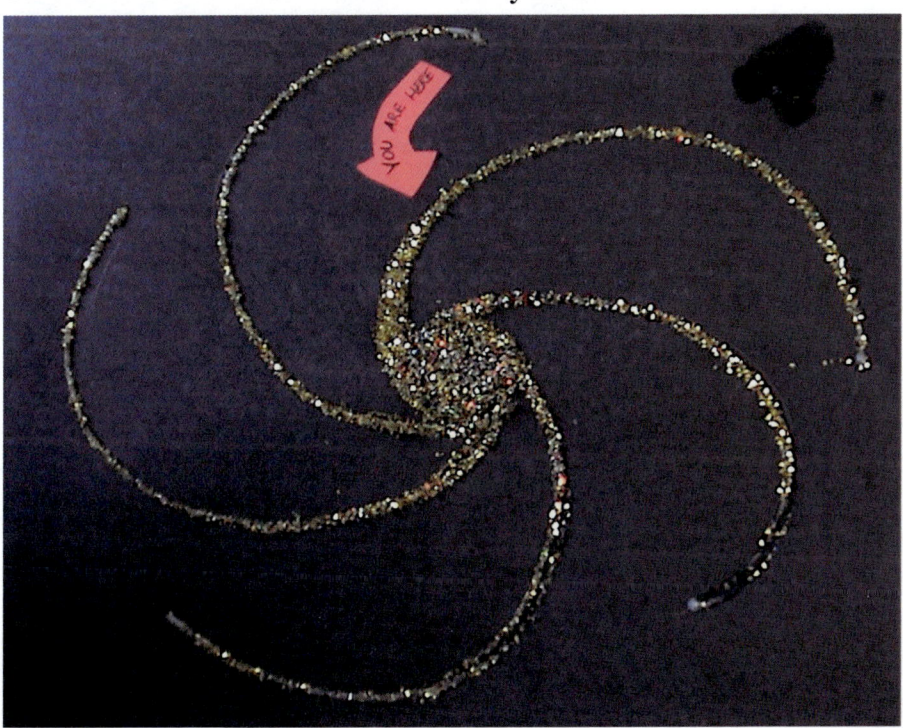

Writer's Workshop

One exosolar system planet people have actually seen with the Hubble Telescope is a planet orbiting the star Fomalhaut.

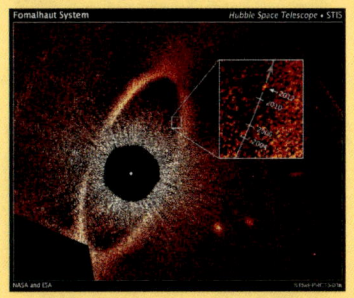

Astronomers named it Fomalhaut b. That's a terrible name! What would you name a planet you discovered? Draw a picture of your planet, give it a name, and write a description of what it's like there. How hot is it? Can anything live there? Are there plants there? Is there water? How many moons?

Fabulous Fact

Before scientists begin an experiment, they decide what they think will happen and they write it down. This is the hypothesis.

Sometimes scientists are right, but sometimes they are wrong. A good scientist will learn and change his hypothesis. He will redesign his experiments. A good scientist is very honest.

33

MESOPOTAMIA - MAPS & GLOBES - PLANETS - CAVE PAINTINGS

Famous Folks

The first person to figure out that the earth is round and circles the sun was a Greek named Aristarchus who lived from 310-230 BC.

Galileo (1564-1642) still deserves props for bringing the knowledge back to light and braving the church authorities to publish his knowledge. Go find out more about Aristarchus and Galileo.

Portrait of Galileo by Justus Sustermans, 1636

Additional Layer

The sun is a nearly perfect sphere and is made of hot plasma and gravitational fields.

It's so big that it accounts for more than 99% of the mass of the solar system.

☺ ☺ ☺ EXPEDITION: Seeing the Milky Way

Go out into the country on a dark, clear night. Make sure you're away from city lights to see the Milky Way. Our solar system is in one arm of the Milky Way, so from our vantage point we can see a cross view of the rest of the galaxy. It's a bright splash across the sky running roughly from north to south in the summer time.

☺ ☺ EXPERIMENT: Sun Spots and Solar Flares

Point a telescope at the sun. The other end of the telescope (which you would normally look through) should be aimed at a sheet of white paper. Focus the telescope until you can see the round surface of the sun on the paper. If sunspots are present you'll see dark spots. If a major solar flare occurs you'll see that too.

Learn more about solar flares and their effect on the earth. They cause the aurora borealis and aurora australis. They can also cause dangerous radiation, which our atmosphere mostly protects us from. This poses a major complication when it comes to the colonizing of the Moon or Mars, which do not have adequate atmospheres. Solar flares are also the cause of the periodic global heating and cooling of the earth. With the telescope trained carefully on your sheet of paper, trace the outline of the sun and any sun spots.

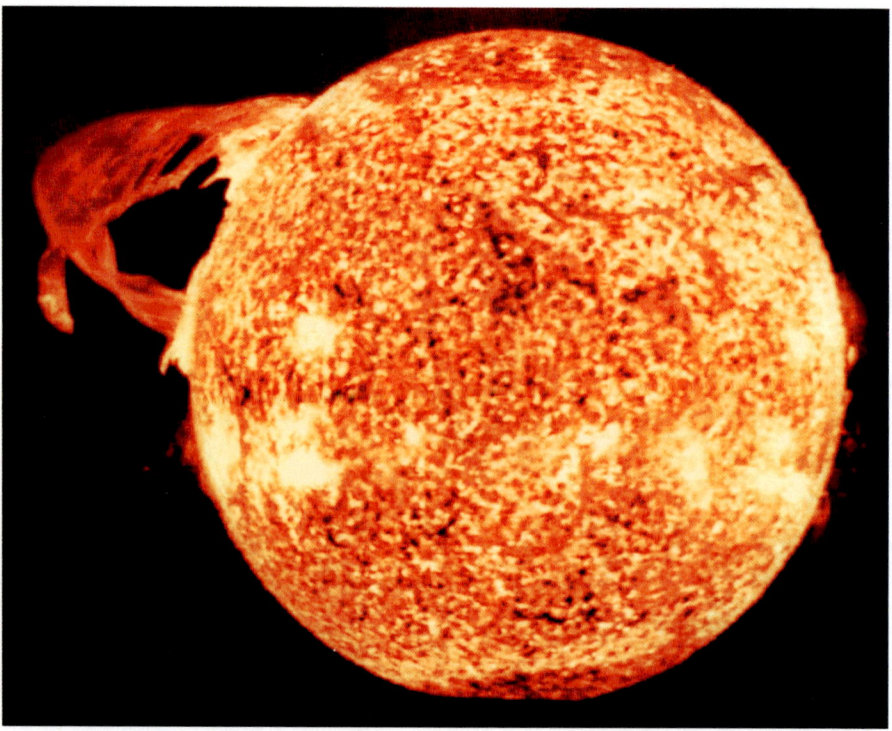

☺ EXPLORATION: My Place in The Universe

Create a diagram showing your place within the Universe. Write the words and draw some pictures to accompany each item. It

MESOPOTAMIA - MAPS & GLOBES - PLANETS - CAVE PAINTINGS

would include these:

Me --> Earth --> Solar System --> Milky Way Galaxy --> Cluster of Galaxies --> Universe

😊 😊 😊 EXPEDITION: Kepler Space Telescope
This is an armchair expedition that uses http://kepler.nasa.gov/, NASA's website about the Kepler telescope and its search for habitable, earth-size planets. It is full of information about what the telescope is finding, and even includes a Kepler Planet Count widget that shows how many extra-solar planets Kepler has discovered so far.

😊 😊 EXPLORATION: Coloring Book of the Planets
You can get a printable coloring book of the planets at www.layers-of-learning.com/planets-coloring-book. Each page has a picture of the planet to color, a spot to practice writing the planet's name, and a few facts about each one. For young ones the coloring and tracing may be enough. Older kids can use the coloring book pages as chapter dividers in a book they create about the planets. In between each one they can include essays about what they learn about each planet, experiment write-ups, and more.

Fabulous Fact

Moons can be found around many planets, not just Earth. Mars has two: Phobos and Deimos.

Mars' moon, Phobos

Neptune has fourteen moons. The other gas giants all have several moons of their own.

Teaching Tip

Sometimes as teachers we want to have all the answers, but sometimes the most beautiful answer is "I don't know."

The truth is, there's a lot we just don't know. And that's okay. If the answer is out there, we'll go find it together. If it's not, there's a lesson there too. The scientists at NASA are always learning new things that no one knew before. The quest for knowledge is just beginning.

T.S. Elliot said, "We shall not cease from exploration, and the end of all our exploring will be to arrive where we started and know the place for the first time."

MESOPOTAMIA - MAPS & GLOBES - PLANETS - CAVE PAINTINGS

THE ARTS: CAVE PAINTINGS

Additional Layer

Art from ancient times has been found all over the world and gives us a lot of insight into what specific civilizations were like. It has been found in places like Korea, China, Japan, India, Mesopotamia, Iran, Central America, Europe, and throughout Asia. Choose a location and learn more about the specific kinds of artifacts that have been found there.

This is a rock painting of a turtle.

Writer's Workshop

Imagine you are an ancient cave dweller, and write a day-in-the-life story about what one of your days is like. Remember that you don't have a grocery store to buy your food in. You can't pick up your clothes from a local mall. There's no builder or architect to help you build your shelter. What is life like for you? How do you spend most of your time?

Very early on the desire to create images manifested itself among mankind. Some of the world's earliest artists were cave painters. Cave walls are filled with anciently drawn charging buffalo, leaping deer, wild horses, and other animals. It is thought that the painters believed making these pictures would bring them good luck in hunting. They used burned wood, soil, and leaves to create strong outlines and muted colors. Many of them can still be seen all these thousands of years later.

One of the most famous cave paintings is from France in Lascaux. It's famous because it is a big network of caves that has almost 2,000 figures painted within them. Most of the pictures are of animals, but there are also human figures and some geometric symbols. One section is called "The Great Hall of the Bulls" that has a painting of a bull that is 17 feet long, the biggest ancient character that has ever been found. The cave art was discovered by four teenagers in 1940. The art has lasted through thousands of years, but just since 1940 it has deteriorated a lot because of all the visitors, the modern lighting that has been installed, and the air conditioning system. The art has become more faded and mold is growing rampantly in the cave now. From time to time the caves have been closed to visitors because of the damage.

We often hear about Lascaux because of its size and large number of paintings, but it was certainly not the only example of

MESOPOTAMIA - MAPS & GLOBES - PLANETS - CAVE PAINTINGS

this ancient art. In fact, cave paintings have been found across the globe, on every continent except Antarctica. Caves were also likely not the only surfaces used for painting, but because they are so well protected from the elements, those are the images that have survived all these years. Cave art was an early forerunner to the art of the Egyptians, Greeks, and Romans, who all did their fair share of painting directly on walls as well.

☺ ☺ ☻ **EXPEDITION: Lascaux**
This virtual expedition will take you inside the Lascaux Caves in France. You'll feel like you're really inside the cave and see firsthand the beautiful earth-toned art of the ancients. www.lascaux.culture.fr.

☺ ☺ ☻ **EXPLORATION: World of Cave Art**
When you go visit an art gallery you will often receive an exhibition brochure with pictures within the exhibit. Create your own World of Cave Art Brochure. Include a page for Europe, Asia, Africa, Australia, North America, and South America. Next to each example of cave art write a brief description of the painting. Can you find any interesting differences between the pieces?

☺ ☺ ☻ **EXPLORATION: The Care and Keeping of Art**
There are a couple of easy methods for storing art projects that kids make. The first thing every budding artist should have is a simple sketchbook. Find one with heavier weight paper and spiral binding. Let your artists decorate the front. It will be used in many of the art units. Spend time now at the very beginning of your art journey to get your portfolio ready and personalized.

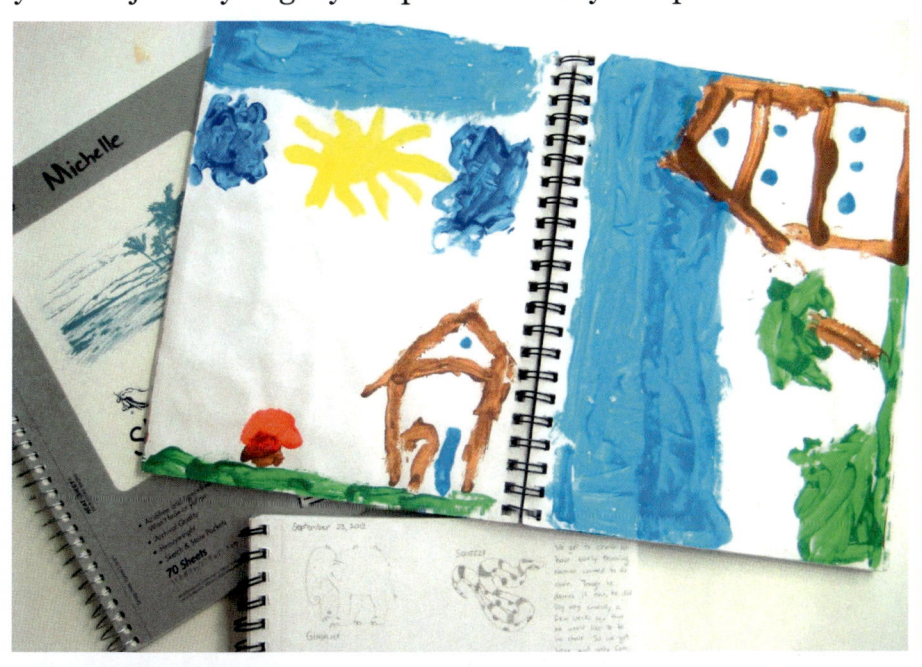

Additional Layer
Some scientists believe that some of the cave paintings at Lascaux actually depict a star map. Look it up on the internet and find out what evidence they've found of this.

Teaching Tip
How-to-draw books are excellent art teachers. Kids see how simple shapes and lines make up complex figures, become better at manipulating those lines to create what they want. They begin to see line and shapes in objects around them that they want to draw.

Encourage your kids in their drawing ability by purchasing a few such books for them. Draw with them. It's a great way to spend time together. You can also find "how to draw" anything on the web.

Mesopotamia - Maps & Globes - Planets - Cave Paintings

Fabulous Fact

Along with the many paintings of animals and hunters, archaeologists have also found markings that they believe to be a game similar to tic-tac-toe.

Teaching Tip

Try starting off this lesson by building a "cave" out of blankets.

When they see it, the kids will be excited and immediately interested in the lesson. But before they go in the cave to create their art talk about what caves are like and what spelunkers (cave explorers) need to be safe.

Then make paper head lamps and paper "flashlights." Art, geology, crafts, and life skills combined into one fun lesson.

You can also create an artist's portfolio in either a binder or an accordion file. If the art is too big or bulky (like a sculpture or a mural), just take a picture to put into the portfolio.

You may also want to have a gallery to display especially well done pieces. This can be as simple as a your fridge, a bulletin board, or a bare wall that you don't mind putting tacks in.

☺ ☺ ☺ **EXPLORATION: Cave Paintings**

First, gather your materials. You'll need:

- a brown paper grocery bag
- a pencil
- charcoal pencil (or a wide black marker)
- paintbrushes
- tempera paints (black, red, orange, brown, gold)

Now prepare your "cave wall" by crumpling up the brown paper bag so it looks rough and worn. Beat it up! You can even spray it with water from a spray bottle (don't soak it) and then dry it with a hair dryer. Now use a pencil to draw simple animals, plants, and people. You can make stick figures or use simple shapes (like squares, circles, diamonds, ovals, etc.) to make the figures.

Go over the pencil lines with the charcoal or marker, making lines that are nice and thick. Then add details like antlers, eyes, tails, and ears with black tempera paint. Once those details have dried (should just take a minute or two), paint the whole thing with the earth toned tempera paints. For a twist on this project try painting your cave art on real rocks.

Mesopotamia - Maps & Globes - Planets - Cave Paintings

☺ ☻ **EXPLORATION: Natural Art**

In ancient days you couldn't just head over to the store to buy your art supplies. What would you use to create art? You don't have paper, so get a nice, flat stone instead. Now try to find some things like soil, leaves, dandelions, and a charred stick to draw with. I turned my kids loose in the back yard on this project and challenged them to find things they could use as paints, brushes, and drawing implements. Soon dandelions, charcoal, and branches were all being used to make natural art.

EXPLANATION: Art Elements

Throughout each art unit, point out the specific elements of art that are important within that unit. Here are the basic elements:

Line: any continuous mark within the artwork. Lines could be straight, curved, organic; any continuous line in any shape

Shape: an enclosed figure, can be geometric or organic

Form: a 3-D shape, like a cube, cylinder, or sphere

Color: this element has 3 properties — hue (the name of the color), intensity (the strength or brightness), and value (the lightness or darkness). Different colors can portray various moods and feelings within art.

Texture: refers to the surface or "feel." This can be real texture (which could be felt by rubbing your hand along the piece) or simulated (the appearance of texture without the actual bumpiness).

Space: the area around, above, or within objects in the art.

For example, when looking at ancient art, it would be important to point out the role that texture played within cave art. Ancient artists used the natural texture of the stone as they created their pictures. Within the caves there are many animals that are 3-D because the painters used the bumps in the walls to draw on and give the animals shape. Also, you may point out the use of color within the cave paintings. What hues did they use? Why would earth tones be the hues they used primarily?

☺ ☻ **EXPLORATION: Textured Rubbings**

Texture is one of the important elements of art, and it played a big role in cave art. The surfaces the artists were using were not perfectly smooth canvases or sheets of paper. They utilized the texture of the walls to make their art come alive. Sometimes artists don't have real texture to work with, so they simulate it. Let's look a little closer at texture. . .

Fabulous Fact

Natural materials were used as paints. The three main types of pigments used by the first artists were yellow ocher, red ocher (both from colored clay), and black from manganese.

Memorization Station

Memorizing all of the elements of art will be useful in all your art studies. It will allow you to understand and be able to describe what an artist has done and the tools they've used. These elements also give us a common language to discuss pieces – one that we all understand.

Additional Layer

We can see what kinds of animals lived in the times and places of the artists who drew them by looking at their art. For example, there are fossils and coinciding cave pictures of species like the cave lion and the woolly mammoth.

Painting by Charles R. Thomas (1920)

Mesopotamia - Maps & Globes - Planets - Cave Paintings

Fabulous Fact

All things have texture, not just bumpy things. Smooth is just as much a texture as rough.

Additional Layer

The Cueva de las Manos (or Cave of Hands) in Argentina is thought to represent a rite of passage. Young boys could mark their hand print upon coming of age. Most of the hand prints are left hands, which indicates that they were mostly right-handed and would have used their dominant hand to hold the paint.

Photo by Maxima20, CC license, Wikimedia

Does your culture have any common rites of passage as you grow up? Do you have any that are specific to your family?

Definitions

Pictographs are made with paint on a rock wall.

Petroglyphs are made by chipping away the stone to leave a picture. They are also on rock walls.

You can feel things that have texture. They may be bumpy, fuzzy, or jagged. They can be tactile (you can actual feel them) or visual (they look rough, bumpy, or some other texture, even though they aren't really). Artists use tricks to make smooth, flat paper look bumpy and textured. Gather these things:

- crayons
- paper
- anything you can do a rubbing of (paperclips, rubber bands, toothpicks, staples, coins, sandpaper)

Place the objects under your paper and rub the crayons across the top of the paper. This will create a rubbing of the object underneath. When you feel the paper it is smooth to the touch, but it appears to have texture.

☺ ☺ ☺ EXPLORATION: Pet Rocks

To give the experience of what it feels like to paint on rough textures, paint a pet rock. Before you begin, take a look at the overall shape of your rock. Look at the indentations, shapes, and textures of your rock. Try to "see" an animal in it. A long skinny rock might make a better snake than a hippopotamus. Decide on an animal that suits your rock's shape, and paint it. Put it out in your garden for everyone to enjoy.

☺ ☺ ☺ EXPLORATION: My Day in Stick Figures

Figures on cave paintings were not the elaborate, realistic paintings of the Renaissance, nor were they the emotional and sym-

MESOPOTAMIA - MAPS & GLOBES - PLANETS - CAVE PAINTINGS

bolic pieces of the Romantic period. They were not as vibrant as modern day art. They had their own style though. Their trademark was a different kind of symbolism. It was telling stories in a simple way – much like the symbolism in our own alphabet. We use simple symbols, letters, combined together to create meaning. We can use them to relay information and tell stories. They used simple figures to convey stories and messages too. It became their written language in a sense. Use the printable from the end of this unit to get some ideas, then tell your own simple story of your day using figures that you create.

Fabulous Facts

This painting of cattle is from Africa.

This is a red feather serpent god from Mexico.

☺ ☺ ☺ **EXPEDITION: Pictographs and Petroglyphs in Person**
Pictographs and petroglyphs can be found all over the United States and Canada in every state and province. Visit some near you. You can see a big long list of places to go at www.layers-of-learning.com/pictographs-and-petroglyphs.

Look for more examples online. It's fascinating to see many at once.

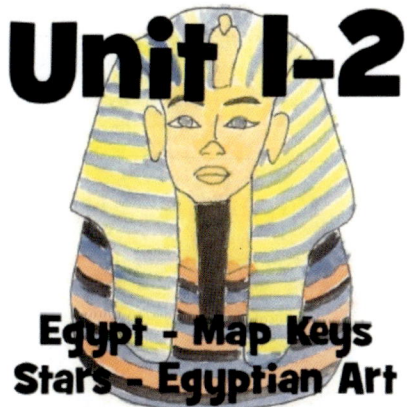

Coming up next . . .
Unit 1-2
Egypt - Map Keys
Stars - Egyptian Art

MESOPOTAMIA - MAPS & GLOBES - PLANETS - CAVE PAINTINGS

My ideas for this unit:

Title: _____ **Topic:** _____

_____
_____
_____
_____
_____
_____
_____
_____
_____
_____

Title: _____ **Topic:** _____

_____
_____
_____
_____
_____
_____
_____
_____
_____
_____

Title: _____ **Topic:** _____

_____
_____
_____
_____
_____
_____
_____
_____
_____
_____

MESOPOTAMIA - MAPS & GLOBES - PLANETS - CAVE PAINTINGS

Title: _____ **Topic:** _____

_____
_____
_____
_____
_____
_____
_____
_____
_____
_____
_____

Title: _____ **Topic:** _____

_____
_____
_____
_____
_____
_____
_____
_____
_____
_____
_____

Title: _____ **Topic:** _____

_____
_____
_____
_____
_____
_____
_____
_____
_____
_____
_____

Fertile Crescent

The Fertile Crescent was a perfect spot for people to settle and create a civilization. There was plenty of water and fertile land for farming due to the nearby Tigris and Euphrates Rivers. This area is sometimes called the cradle of civilization because, like a cradle for a baby, it was a place where cities and government were first nurtured.

FERTILE CRESCENT
Assyria
Akkad
Phoenicia
Syrian Desert
Sumer

Layers of Learning

The Fertile Crescent

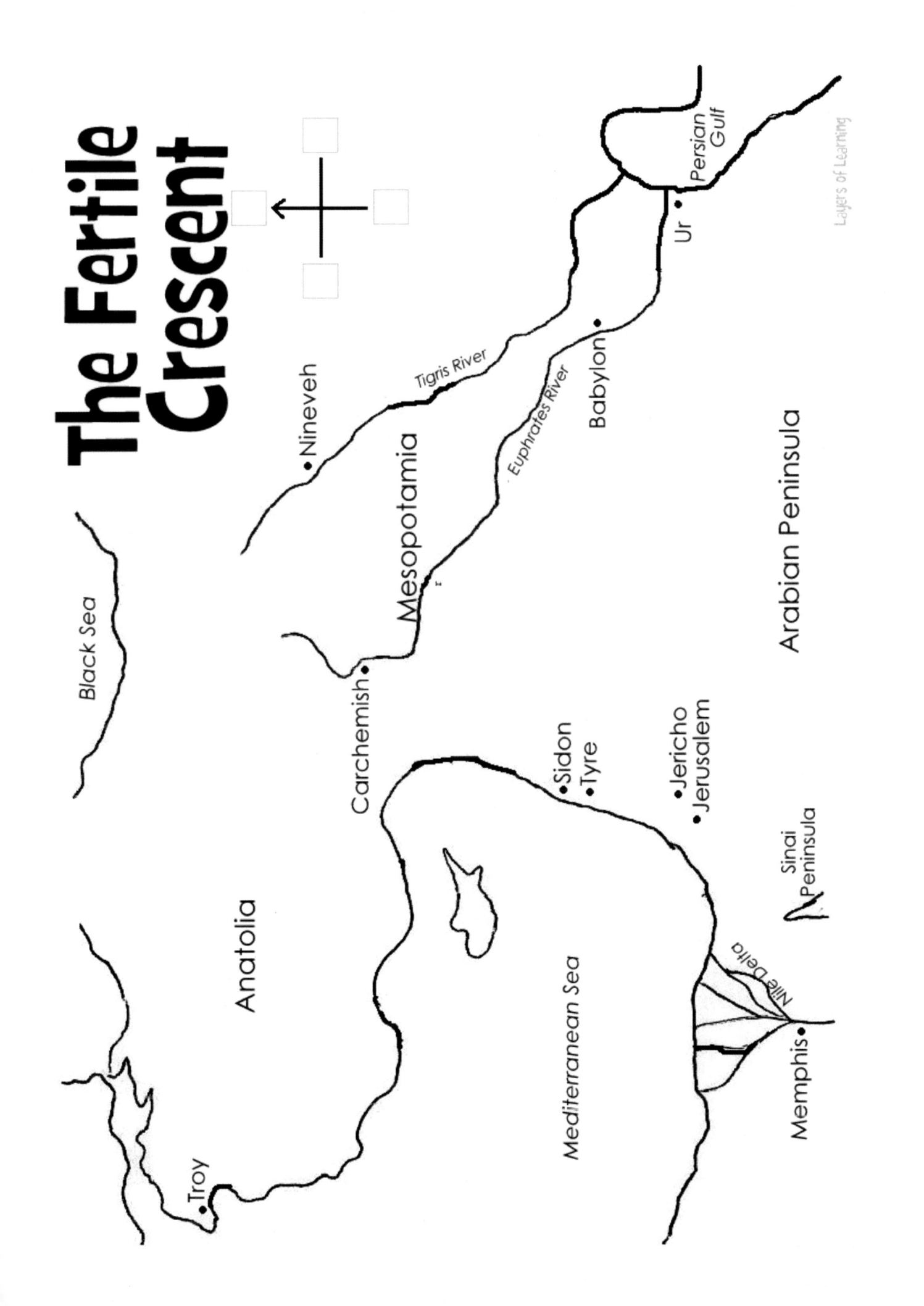

- Black Sea
- Troy
- Anatolia
- Mediterranean Sea
- Carchemish
- Sidon
- Tyre
- Jericho
- Jerusalem
- Sinai Peninsula
- Nile Delta
- Memphis
- Nineveh
- Mesopotamia
- Tigris River
- Euphrates River
- Babylon
- Ur
- Persian Gulf
- Arabian Peninsula

Layers of Learning

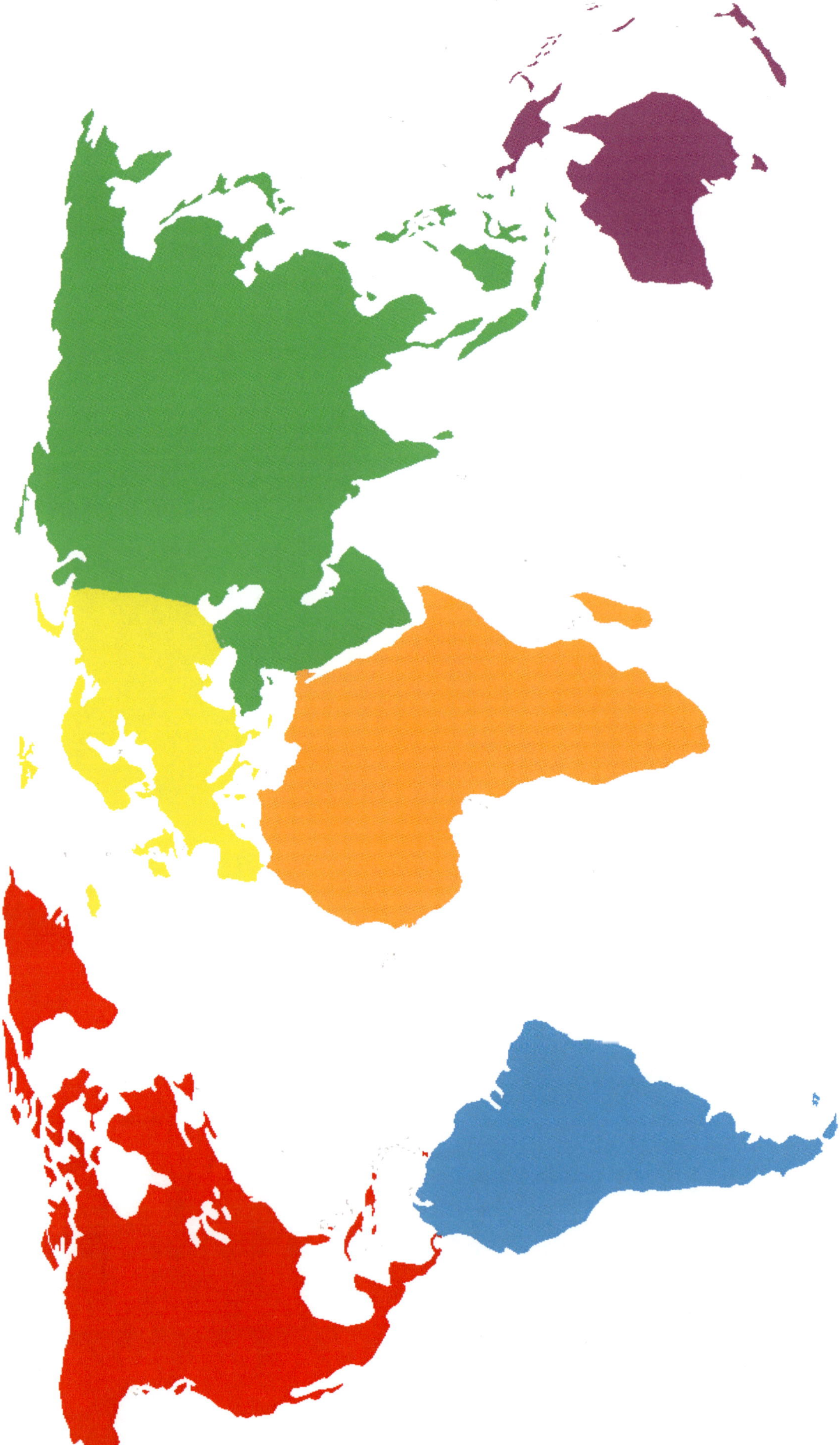

Travel Brochure

(name of place)

Fun Things To Do

-
-
-
-
-

I would like to vacation here because…

Layers of Learning

Where I Live

by: _____

- -

Planet

My home, my city, my state, and my country are on the planet Earth.

Home

I live in this home.

- -

Country

My home, my city and my state are in the country of

_____ .

City

My home is in the city of _____ .

- -

State

My home and my city are in the state of

_____ .

City

My home is in the city of _____ .

- -

Province

My home and my city are in the province of

_____ .

Solar System

My home, my city, my state, my country, and my planet are in the solar system.

My Day

Look at the picture symbols of my day.
Can you tell what I did today?

Now draw what you did today.

Layers of Learning

About the Authors

Karen & Michelle . . .
Mothers, sisters, teachers, women who are passionate
about educating kids.
We are dedicated to lifelong learning.

Karen, a mother of four, who has homeschooled her kids for more than eight years with her husband, Bob, has a bachelor's degree in child development with an emphasis in education. She lives in Idaho, gardens, teaches piano, and plays an excruciating number of board games with her kids. Karen is our resident arts expert and English guru {most necessary as Michelle regularly and carelessly mangles the English language and occasionally steps over the bounds of polite society}.

Michelle and her husband, Cameron, have homeschooled their six boys for more than a decade. Michelle earned a bachelors in biology, making her the resident science expert, though she is mocked by her friends for being the Botanist with the Black Thumb of Death. She also is the go-to for history and government. She believes in staying up late, hot chocolate, and a no whining policy. We both pitch in on geography, in case you were wondering, and are on a continual quest for knowledge.

Visit our constantly updated blog for tons of free ideas,
free printables, and more cool stuff for sale:
www.Layers-of-Learning.com

Made in the USA
Middletown, DE
08 January 2024